What people are saying

Transformation happens best when information and interaction collide. That's what I love about Tina Rae's *Devotions for the Artist at Heart*. It combines the power of God's Word with the visceral nature of creative reflection, which has the capacity to yield great results in the life of the reader. This is a great resource for artists or those who are artists at heart and want to grow creatively and spiritually.

—Matt Tommey
Artist, author, and mentor
www.matttommeymentoring.com

The connection between art and spirituality is often reduced to a dry philosophical discussion. In *Devotions for the Artist at Heart*, Tina Rae brings this link to life, inspiring joy in those of us who simply want to use our artistic talents to glorify God and bless others. Weaving together personal anecdotes, creative exercises, and spiritual insights, Tina—a remarkable artist herself—reminds us that we've been made in the image of a creative God and we can celebrate that! I'm excited to dig into this book.

—Ann-Margret Hovsepian
Author and illustrator of *Restore My Soul*

Tina Rae has created a devotional book unlike any I have encountered! I'm convinced everyone moving through this devotional will discover inspiration, encouragement, and challenge to respond to the leading of the Holy Spirit in artistic ways. I appreciate the honesty and vulnerability from which Tina shares her own spiritual journey and leads readers to engage in fresh ways with our Creator God.

—Rev. Tanya Yuen
Children and Family Ministries Associate

In Tina Rae's careful hands, this book is more than your standard devotional. It's a deep sharing of the Artist at work in her life, unfolding page by page as she invites you to take the time to read Scripture and then create art.

Page by page, you'll sit safely in the presence of Jesus and listen, see, draw, colour, paint… and one day in His presence you'll realize that you too are a work of art that matters… fashioned by God, reflecting His image. Enjoy!

—Renee James
Award-winning writer and editor
Director of Communications and Editor of *live* Magazine
Canadian Baptist Women of Ontario and Quebec

DEVOTIONS FOR THE Artist AT HEART

Get Creative and Draw Your Devotions!

DEVOTIONS FOR THE ARTIST AT HEART

Print ISBN: 978-1-4866-2005-0
eBook ISBN: 978-1-4866-2006-7

Word Alive Press
119 De Baets Street, Winnipeg, MB R2J 3R9
www.wordalivepress.ca

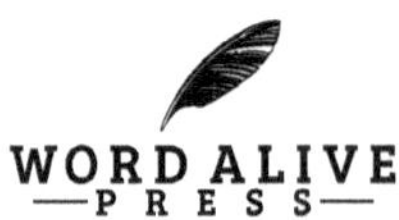

Cataloguing in Publication may be obtained through Library and Archives Canada

Contents

Acknowledgements

Creating this book has been an amazing journey from the small promptings to write it, to the affirmations, and through to the editing process. I want to thank those who have supported and encouraged me along the way.

Thank you to Rev. Andrea Chang for listening to God's leading and being His messenger to share such a clear message from Him that I needed to write and share these devotions.

Thank you to those who read through, edited, and gave feedback on my early drafts of the book. It took a lot of time and dedication, so thank you to Debbie, Pastor Phil, Renee, and Ann-Margaret for intentionally setting aside the time and for supporting me along the way.

Thank you to my husband, Geoff, who listened as I worked through how to best express some of these ideas on paper, helped me make grammar decisions, listened to me talk about it endlessly, and also supported me in going ahead to get this book published.

I also appreciate my small group, who allowed me to try out many of these devotions for our weekly art gathering. I particularly appreciate Charlotte for coming to me with the idea to even run this class and for working together with me to teach and inspire people to express their faith through their art.

Thank you to those who are a part of some of these devotions. Your stories are so important, and I am so glad I can share them in a way that highlights both art and faith. I'm glad for your permission to share these stories to encourage people in their artistic worship and understanding of God.

So many people have encouraged me along the way, and although I cannot mention everyone, if you were one of those people who listened as I spoke about this book and gave me your feedback or encouragement, know that it was greatly appreciated and propelled the launching of this book and these stories to be shared.

Introduction

I have several distinct memories of how art has made a deep and profound impact on my life. Many of these are simple moments in time, but they have stayed with me for years and I have drawn upon them to motivate me as an artist. Some have been good, and others have had a negative impact, but both types of memories have helped motivate me to get where I am today.

One of my earliest memories was a good one. When I was in Grade One, I remember learning about artist and author Barbara Reid, who illustrated her book using plasticine to create beautiful images. In response to our study of the book, our teacher challenged us to create images from plasticine.

With the theme of spring in mind, I chose to make a robin. I worked hard to create the best robin I could. I specifically remember wanting to capture the texture of the feathers. I found a straw and inserted it at a slight angle so that the end of the straw formed an oblong oval shape to represent the robin's feathers.

I remember feeling proud of my creation, and I remember being praised for my work. I even recall one of my peers telling me that I should be an artist when I grew up, which made me feel really good about what I had created.

Unfortunately, I also have sharp and contrasting stories that detract from encouraging moments like the one I just mentioned. I did continue to create, and I loved my art classes, but there were a few moments of discouragement. One of them brought me to tears.

In high school, I was asked to create a fireplace for a school play. I envisioned what I thought it should look like and chose an impressionistic style rather than a more precise and realistic representation. With an impressionistic style, the lines were less defined. I thought, since it was being viewed from a distance, it would look good that way. My teacher thought otherwise and said it couldn't be used. It was disposed of and I had to start over.

I worked on the new fireplace but did so with a saddened and heavy heart. I feared creating anything for anyone ever again. I feared others would also react negatively, even before I tried to create something. Artwork became a private endeavor for me, and when I later got busy with college and having kids it became a low priority.

Moments like these have set back my creative process and can continue to hold me back. Thankfully, I've had enough positive experiences and encouragement through my faith that I am able to continue my artist's journey and move forward.

Many of us have these memories. We have moments of joy, brought down by moments of deep discouragement, and sometimes it's difficult to move forward from them.

My hope in creating this book is that you may be inspired to take steps forward in connecting with both your faith and your creative process. You may be in a good place and these devotions may further encourage you, but if you come from a place of discouragement or uncertainty about your artistic skill, I pray that this book will help you reconnect with the artistic part of your soul.

As I transitioned out of my season of creating little artwork, and as my kids grew older, I've had more and more opportunities to get back into my artwork. I have continued to paint and interact with many people in art circles, feeling a strong tug to consider how I could bridge my faith and art together.

One day I had the thought to write a devotional with art inspirations following each reading. I'd never heard of a devotional like that and it really excited me to consider.

The first person I told about this project questioned whether there would actually be a market for a book like this, and I put the idea aside. Fortunately, I've felt continual promptings to revisit this idea and eventually decided to go for it. This book may or may not be a bestseller, but sometimes you need to take a step forward to see what God will do with what He has called you to do.

This book was written to help inspire people of all levels of artistic skill to connect with God through their art. Nearly all art challenges can be completed with a set of coloured pencils, but they're open ended enough that many types of art materials could be used. For those who don't consider themselves artistically gifted, this may be more of a personal journal, but for those who are aspiring artists, or even experts, this book may be an encouragement or a launching point.

THIS BOOK WAS WRITTEN TO HELP INSPIRE PEOPLE OF ALL LEVELS OF ARTISTIC SKILL

Each devotion has an art challenge. You should be able to sketch right in this book to help start your artistic journey for the day. Don't feel that you must respond to the devotion solely through the art challenge. If God inspires another thought in your mind, feel free to explore that, but if you struggle with inspiration, the art challenges are there to help get you started.

The devotions are designed to be short and should take approximately five minutes each, but feel free to spend as much or as little time as you wish on the art portion. If you need a few days to work on something, continue working on one devotion for as much time as you have available. Give your artistic ideas all the time they need to fully develop.

I pray that these devotions will help provide insight into God's Word from an artistic eye, but also encourage you on your walk of faith. May God bless you as you seek to express your faith through art.

Whatever you do, work at it with all your heart, as though you were working for the Lord and not for people.

—Colossians 3:23, GNT

Inspired by Creation

READ GENESIS 1:1–25

In the beginning God created the heavens and the earth.

—Genesis 1:1

Have you ever read a book where the author painted such a vivid picture that you could imagine exactly what they were talking about? Not all the details were there, but enough was shared through words on the page that you could fill the spaces in between to picture exactly what the author was describing.

Some Bible passages lend themselves well to imagery and others need to be studied more before an image comes to mind. Genesis 1 is one of those descriptive chapters that seems to overflow with imagery. We begin with *"In the beginning God created the heavens and the earth"* before getting a description of the world God creates. The light and darkness are separated, the skies are separated from the waters, and then God forms dry land. We read of the heavenly bodies and then of the many animals God filled the world with.

Every detail is not described in full, but an image comes to mind, and I can imagine exactly what is being described. The basic details leave room for the imagination, and the images I see are different each time I read this passage. Sometimes I think of the grandeur of a galaxy, the soft glow of a sunset, or the amazing complexity of an individual animal God has placed on the earth. The beauty of the image inspires me to contemplate it more and appreciate what God has created.

Art Challenge

Read Genesis 1 and consider what images come to mind. Use this page to draw the image. While you're drawing, think about whether there's something God is saying to you. A specific image can inspire you to do something as simple as praise God, but be open to the idea that God could be saying something more to you.

Let Go of the Stress

READ PHILIPPIANS 4:6–7, MATTHEW 6:25–34

Can any one of you by worrying add a single hour to your life?

—Matthew 6:27

I am often asked how I have the time to create art. I'm married, a mother of two, and I hold a full-time job and that on its own takes a great deal of time. However, my question in return is more like, how could I not make time to create art?

I spent several years when my kids were young creating very little art. I did some scrapbooking and there were occasional moments when I could be crafty with my job, but during that time, when the pressures of life piled up, I needed a better outlet. To help me relax, I placed a greater focus on some of the things I loved. For me, that was playing baseball and creating art.

So the reason I have time is that I've decided to intentionally set it aside to create art. I love creating something new, I love new creative challenges, and I believe that creating art is calming for me.

If you haven't heard about the mental health benefits of creating art, you need to know that creating art is a proven way to reduce stress. One published study found that seventy-five percent of participants had lowered cortisol levels after participating in forty-five minutes of creative art expression.[1] And for those of you who may argue that you aren't good at art, another article stated that creating simple stick figure drawings were also found to lower stress levels![2]

In the Bible, we read that we should not worry about anything. We're asked to come to God in prayer and trust in Him because He will take care of us. Prayer and faith are essential and important, and so is rest. God gave us the Sabbath as well, a day to put our stresses aside. We need to remember that God gave us many tools to help us to worry less.

As you get creative with your devotions today, come before God with all your worries and lay them before Him. Set them aside as you trust in Him.

---

1 Girija Kaimal, Kendra Ray, and Juan Muniz, "Reduction of Cortisol Levels and Participants' Responses Following Art Making," *Art Therapy*, Volume 33, Issue 2 (2016), 74–80.

2 Drexel University, "Stress-Related Hormone Cortisol Lowers Significantly After Just 45 Minutes of Art Creation," *Psypost*. June 16, 2016 (https://www.psypost.org/2016/06/skill-level-making-art-reduces-stress-hormone-cortisol-43362).

Art Challenge

What came to mind when you read today's passage? Draw something related to the passage or create something that brings you joy. If you love doodling, draw simple figures and shapes. If you enjoy a more abstract style, try something like a collage or pour art. If attention to fine details brings you joy, spend time working on a realistic sketch.

Created in His Image

READ GENESIS 1:26–31

Then God said, "Let us make human beings in our image…"

—Genesis 1:26, NLT

Have you ever really thought about what it means that we are created in God's image? I often think about the physical qualities we have and how they must have a similar appearance to God, and I often forget that we are also created in God's likeness. Being made in God's likeness means that we not only have some similar physical qualities, but we were created to have some similar characteristics to God.

As an artist, I love to consider how our creativity is a reflection of God. He created the whole world and paid attention to every minute detail. He cares about every leaf, every bird, and every blade of grass. He made the world from nothing, and the beauty of this world takes my breath away, especially when I see rainbows, thunderstorms, or a sunset! God was creative in the beginning and continues to be creative to this day.

If God created all of us in His image, it follows that we too are called to be creative. We bring honour to God through taking a blank page and using it to reflect the world we see around us. God loves it when we make something new, create something that tells a story, produce something that expresses our emotion, or design something that brings beauty and meaning to someone's life. We should embrace our call to be creative.

Art Challenge

God created us in His image and calls us to be creative. Use the space provided to contemplate the part of the creation story that focuses on how God created humankind. Create images or write words that represent the creative aspects of who God made you to be.

Note: If you want a more detailed art activity to help you reflect on who God has called you to be, visit "Creative Reflection" in the Detailed Art Challenge Activities section at the end of this book.

Scripture Meditation

READ 1 KINGS 19:11–13

> *And after the fire came a gentle whisper. When Elijah heard it, he pulled his cloak over his face and went out and stood at the mouth of the cave.*
>
> —1 Kings 19:12–13

The first time I heard about this type of scripture meditation, I found it difficult to understand.

Additionally, upon learning the Latin term, *lectio divina*, I was uncertain if this was something that would be beneficial for me. However, the person who shared it with me read a certain scripture multiple times, allowing for time to contemplate the meaning of the verse between repetitions. Being the impatient person I can be, I thought, *I heard it the first time, so why do I need to hear it again?*

Over time, and through gaining more insight and patience into this practice, I have come to better understand its value. It helps me to think about words that grab my attention, to think about why the words seem to come to mind, and to contemplate what God might be saying to me.

Sometimes these words aren't just words for me; they draw a picture in my mind. The words themselves might be written in a certain font which communicates a feeling. They might be jarring or flowing, depending on what I hear in the passage, or they might bring to mind an actual image. When an image comes to mind, I pay attention. I'm learning to write down the details of these images and turn them into visual representations of the scripture. If I revisit that image, I find that it can grow and develop into something more, but I'm always centred on the Scripture that inspired it.

Note that many of the following devotionals can be approached in this manner. Although I suggest art challenges, you may be prompted by God just through reading the scripture. Feel free to respond to the devotional as the Lord leads.

If you would like a more detailed instructional for two different passages, visit the Detailed Art Challenge Activities at the end of this book. They were included to help get a beginning artist started.

Art Challenge

With any passage, read it three times. Today, read 1 Kings 19:11–13. Pause after each reading to contemplate what might stand out to you. Take time to pray about it. Write down the words or draw the images that come to mind on this page.

God Values Creativity

READ EXODUS 35:30–35

...and he has filled him with the Spirit of God, with wisdom, with understanding, with knowledge and with all kinds of skills—to make artistic designs for work in gold, silver and bronze...

—Exodus 35:31–32

Have you ever visited old Catholic churches in Europe? The churches are beautiful. Attention was paid to the form, colour, and aesthetics. There are some famous churches you may know of, like the masterfully painted Michelangelo's Sistine Chapel ceiling, or the intricate and colourful rose stained-glass windows in the Notre-Dame cathedral, which amazingly survived a recent fire in 2019.[3] There are so many other churches you may not know about that have also been created with amazing artistry and architecture in mind.

Through different periods of time, churches have been built with varying degrees of visual appeal, form, and function. Unfortunately, sometimes people were afraid to make something too beautiful because they thought it might detract from worshipping God. However, I believe that it can actually add to someone's worship experience.

As a child, I can remember moments in church when I just stared at the stained-glass windows and totally missed what was going around me because I was bored. I could have looked at the floor, bothered my siblings, or done something else, totally missing God; however, there were moments when I worshipped God because I was drawn to the architecture and stained-glass windows around me. I was thankful for their colour and the stories pictured in them. I learned many of God's stories through these beautiful windows.

When God instructed the Israelites to build the tabernacle, visual appeal was important to Him too. He didn't only say that the tabernacle was created for efficiency and function; He gifted individuals to make it beautiful. Bezalel and Oholiab were filled with the Spirit of God to make artistic designs and were instructed to use varying colours, to use metals, stones, gems, and wood. God also gave them the ability to teach others how to use these skills and make the tabernacle fit for our God and King.

When someone thinks that creating art detracts from worship, we should challenge that mindset. God gifts and empowers people to make things beautiful. It was a requirement when the tabernacle

---

3 Katie Dangerfield, "Notre Dame Fire: 'Priceless' Stained-Glass Windows May Have Survived Destruction," *Global News*. April 16, 2019 (https://globalnews.ca/news/5172160/notre-dame-fire-stained-glass-windows/).

and temple were built. When you feel inspired to create, remember how important beauty and creativity are to God.

Art Challenge

Incorporate metallic colours into your artwork to highlight or accent a design of your choosing. Consider drawing a building or place where you could worship.

Alternatively, create a design for your own stained-glass window that you could imagine helping you worship God. It could show a Bible story, something God has created, or you could create a patterned window with the colours mentioned in the scripture reading.

Pay It Forward

READ ACTS 1:4–9

…you will be my witnesses in Jerusalem, and in all Judea and Samaria, and to the ends of the earth.

—Acts 1:8

Recently I dropped into a local library with my son. As we passed through the front entrance, something caught his eye and he went over to investigate. Someone had intentionally placed a rock in a unique place, in order to be found by another person. The rock was painted sky-blue and had the words "You are my sunshine" written on it. On the back of the rock was a message that told us we could either keep the rock or rehide it.

If we wanted to know more, or if we wanted to learn about the journey of the rock, we were instructed to visit a Facebook page about kindness rocks.

When we looked at the website, we learned that a person had started creating these rocks in the summer of 2017 with a group of kids. Ever since, she has continued to inspire others to join in on the movement. Every time a new rock is created, it is hidden somewhere in our city to brighten someone's day. Although some are kept, many are rehidden for the next person to find.

The Facebook page lets those who have found a rock know what to do: "Take one if it means something to you… share with a friend who needs some inspiration… It's all about kindness, right? We all could benefit from it. Pay it forward!"[4]

I loved the idea. I loved how excited my son and I were, and we wanted to pay it forward so that the rock he'd found could brighten someone's day just like it had ours. Now someone else could become a part of the journey.

God has asked us to do something similar. He has asked us to share a message that will inspire and change lives. We are to connect with people in a way that will demonstrate to them the hope and joy that Christ can bring to our lives today, and even into the afterlife. It's the kind of message that brings such joy that we want to share it and pay it forward, because the message that Christ gave us to share brightens more than a single moment; it gives us hope for eternity.

---

4 Dawn-Marie Deagle, "Kindness Rocks in London, ON," *Facebook*. Date of access: February 10, 2020 (https://www.facebook.com/groups/142931482956522).

Art Challenge

There are many ways in which we can share our faith, hope, and joy with those around us—and I love that there are artistic ways we can do that too. Make your own kindness or faith rocks. Sketch ideas in the space provided of what you would put on your rocks. When you have a few ideas, find some rocks, paint them, and leave them for someone to find.

Light in the Darkness

READ ISAIAH 9:1–7

> *The people walking in darkness have seen a great light; on those living in the land of deep darkness a light has dawned.*
>
> —Isaiah 9:2

It can be difficult to share some of the dark parts of your personal story. Talking about sadness, death, sin, pain, and the hurt you've walked through isn't easy. We don't like to revisit those memories.

It can be difficult to hear another person's story of darkness, but many times I have resonated with what they shared. At times I've experienced the same hurt and they were able to understand my pain, but the most meaningful part of the experience is the encouragement that comes from knowing that others have worked through the hurt, so I can too.

How unfortunate it would be if we didn't hear these stories. Hiding them could keep others from being encouraged as they work through their own brokenness.

In considering how our difficulties can have value, I'm reminded of a type of artwork that also values brokenness. It's called kintsugi, a form of Japanese art where broken pottery is repaired with gold, which beautifully highlights the imperfections. The gold brings out the history of the object instead of hiding it, because the history, even though it is broken, is valued.[5]

The history of the Israelites is filled with imperfect people who went through some very difficult times and situations, but these stories aren't hidden from us. They are told to remind us of how God has worked to restore His people to a right relationship with Him.

Today's passage contains a foreshadowing of a bright future wherein God will send His Son to save the Israelites—and to save us. Isaiah brought hope to the Israelites. In these prophetic words, God promises to bring His people redemption and deliver them out of their darkness and brokenness by sending His Son to conquer death. Through this, all who believe in Him can experience light and life.

Be encouraged that this promise is not only for the Israelites, but also for us. He offers Jesus's salvation in addition to His comfort so that we too can hope for a bright future.

---

5 "Kintsugi," *Wikipedia*. Date of access: September 9, 2019 (https://en.wikipedia.org/wiki/Kintsugi).

Art Challenge

Consider something you are struggling through in your own life right now and draw images, symbols, and words that represent that struggle. It can be helpful to explore through artwork a difficult situation you're experiencing. Go back over your drawing with gold or yellow paint, or a gold marker, and contemplate the hope you have and can bring to others through this journey.

Stand Out for God

READ ROMANS 12:1–3

> *Do not conform to the pattern of this world, but be transformed by the renewing of your mind.*
>
> —Romans 12:2

In elementary school, we were often taught to paint a certain way, to create realistic art, to use a certain technique, and generally to make art very similar to how the teacher created it. When we followed this formula, we were rewarded with good grades. I've noticed that as adults, many continue to appreciate artwork that follows similar criteria.

In contrast to what many of us were taught, a great deal of valuable artwork in a museum is unique and can be difficult to understand because it doesn't fit the standard we were taught when we were younger. Many collectors of art value unique pieces and will actually pay a high price for it. Because these pieces are so different, they stand out from the average painting and are more valuable.

Sometimes people see the value right away and sometimes it takes time. Did you know that people didn't appreciate Van Gogh's artwork until after his death? His work was so different that people had trouble understanding it. He only sold one painting in his lifetime, but now his work is highly valued.

Creativity and new ideas are often hard to come by, and because they're so rare they have greater value. Sometimes you see the value now, and other times later.

As a follower of Christ, we are to stand out in a positive way. Sometimes that means responding in a situation differently than others would. It can be a difficult thing to do, but God calls us to be different in a way that reflects Christ so that we can bring people to a better understanding of who our loving God and Father is.

Art Challenge

Jim Le Page created a piece of artwork based on this Bible verse.[6] It's simple yet so profound. It consists of a page filled with black dots in an array and one bright blue hexagon. The hexagon stands out in sharp contrast to the many darkened dots, just as we're called to stand out against the crowds of people around us in the world. We are challenged to consider a couple of questions. Do we stand out and represent Christ well? Are we a beacon of light in a world of darkness?

Create a piece of artwork that shows someone or something standing out from the crowd. Consider using a pattern and choose one part of the pattern to stand out by changing it in some way.

6 Jim Le Page, "Word Bible Designs," *Jim LePage.* Date of access: October 5, 2019 (https://www.jimlepage.com/bible-art).

Lessons in Clay

READ JEREMIAH 18:1–6, ISAIAH 64:8

> *Yet you, Lord, are our Father. We are the clay, you are the potter; we are all the work of your hand.*
>
> —Isaiah 64:8

I've recently branched out to try different forms of art, and I found a local clay shop holding pottery classes for only ten dollars. The price was low, because we didn't get to keep the clay, but it was about practicing using a potter's wheel. I was a little disappointed that I wouldn't get to keep my clay creation, because I just knew I would create a masterpiece. Despite this, my daughter and I decided to go because it was a great deal and we'd enjoy the afternoon out together.

We were given basic instruction and then watched the teacher explain the steps of how to create a beautiful pot, which she formed in minutes. She demonstrated techniques and warned us not to be disappointed, because ninety percent of people aren't naturals. It can take a lot of practice. I figured that since I loved art so much, I probably would be a natural.

But I was wrong. I struggled with the most basic part of creating my pot: centring the clay on the potter's wheel.

You see, you have to have the clay exactly in the middle, or else your pot becomes lopsided and easily falls apart. You end up coming into contact with one side of the clay harder than the other as the wheel turns. The wheel turned, and I tried to force the pot towards the centre, but this only ended up making it worse.

I tried so hard, and even the teachers said that I looked frustrated. I was.

Despite my frustration in not making the perfect creation, this exercise gave me a better appreciation of God as our potter. He is the master creator and knows exactly what He's doing. We can try all we want to force ourselves to be the person we want to be, but we'll struggle when we try to do these things on our own. Maybe we'll have some success and our character and circumstances will turn out okay, but many times they can fall apart. If we give ourselves into God's hands, He can centre us and shape us into the beautiful people we are intended to be.

One of the most profound lessons of my pottery experience was that I really needed to let go. I learned some techniques and needed to trust that with the teacher's guidance and teaching I could create my pot. I actually closed my eyes and tried to stop myself from being so critical of my work. I didn't accomplish anything amazing—this was my first experience, after all—but I centered my work and started to get it.

We may need to let go of some of our well laid plans and let God work through us to create the beautiful lives He intends for us. And if we are in God's skilled hands, and we are centred, we may surprise ourselves in terms of what God can make as He works through us to create something amazing.

Art Challenge

Try your hand at using a potter's wheel or create something with clay; or draw something that stands out to you from Isaiah 64:8. If you choose to draw, make something that radiates outward from a centre point, and remember that God should always be at our centre.

Love for Our Father

READ PSALM 108:1–5

I will praise you, Lord, among the nations; I will sing of you among the peoples.

—Psalm 108:3

My high school friend married a man who's in the military. He is often away for training or on assignment, so my friend and her two daughters recently travelled to France to meet him. She shared a picture online of the moment after her daughters had run to embrace their dad. One of the girls made it up into his arms and hugged him so tightly while the younger wrapped herself around his leg in such a way that she would travel with him with every step he took.

This picture made me think about how we approach our heavenly Father. Depending on our relationship with God, we may approach Him in different ways. Will we be passive or distant in meeting Him? Will we shake His hand as we approach, wave hello, or run into His arms with excitement and joy, looking to embrace Him in any way we can?

I imagine David approached God in a similarly enthusiastic way. As you read through the Psalms, many emotions and feelings are represented. We read psalms of praise, lament, wisdom, and thanksgiving, and almost every single one of them has words of praise and hope to give to God our Father. When David praised God, he did so with such joy that you can tell how much he loved our heavenly Father.

Despite difficulties, David turned to God and praised who He is. Take time to consider how you approach God. You may have something you need to work out with Him, but hopefully you can come back to a place where you feel a closeness to God, so you feel able to fully embrace Him with love and joy.

Art Challenge

When reading through today's passage, are there words or verses that stand out to you when reflecting on how you feel about God? If you want to strengthen your joy in the Lord, consider the words or verses that reflect how you would like your love for God to be. Choose the words that stand out to you and write them inside the heart provided. Add images that come to mind that represent these words.

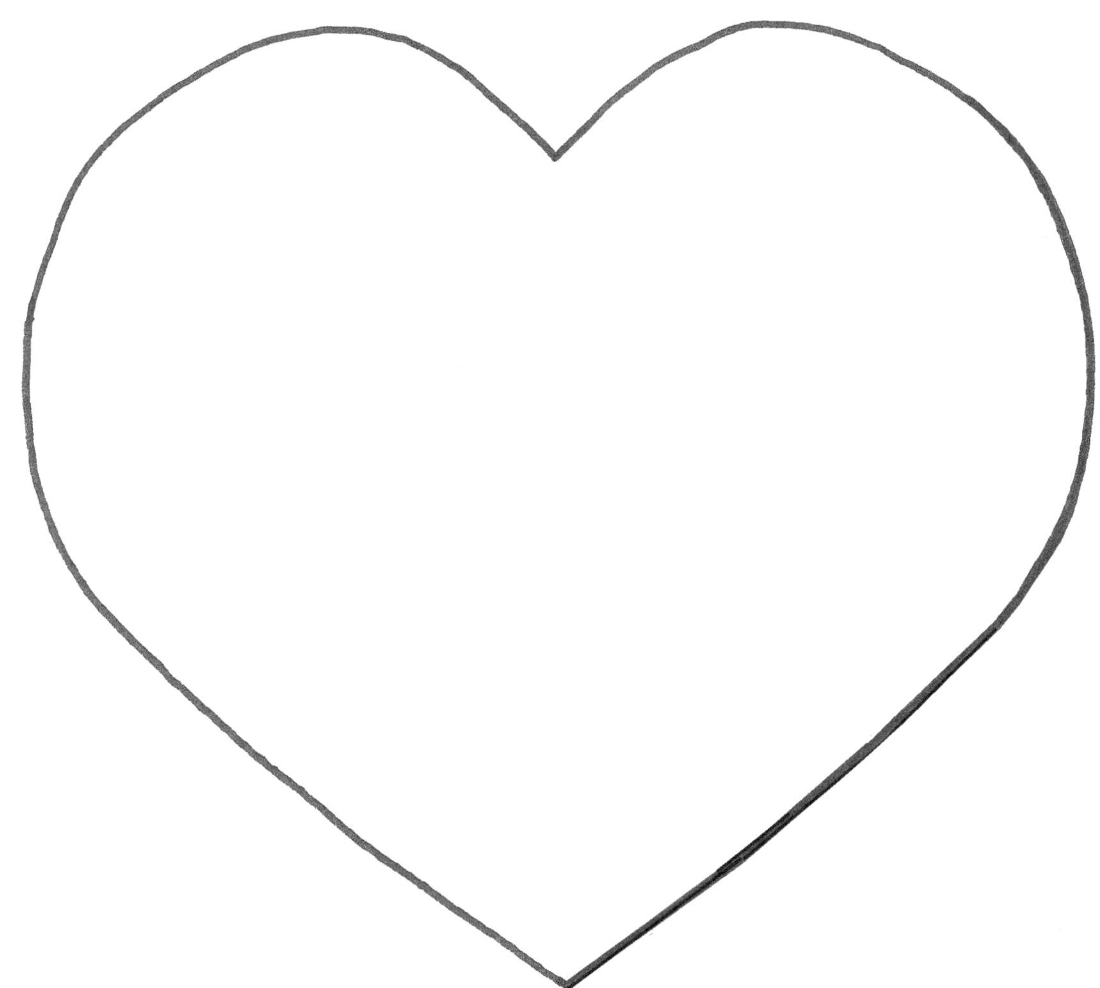

It's a Matter of Perspective

READ 2 TIMOTHY 2:22–26

Again I say, don't get involved in foolish, ignorant arguments that only start fights.

—2 Timothy 2:23, NLT

Pictured in this devotion is the Penrose Staircase.[7] Which direction does the staircase go? Up or down? Are you certain? Your perspective depends on how you look at it, or how you focus on the picture.[8]

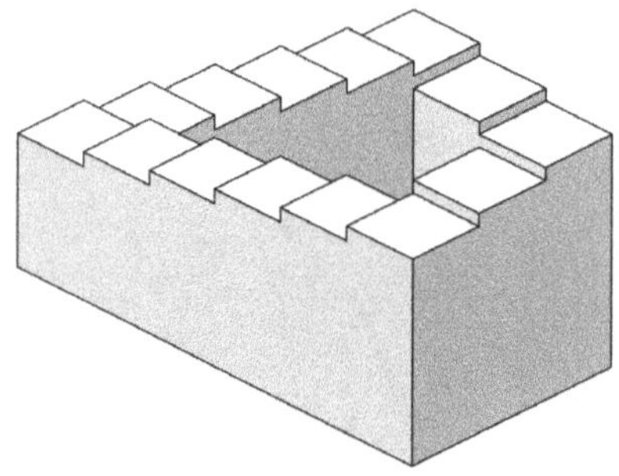

Penrose Staircase

Sometimes people argue over a simple issue like this, and it isn't worth it. Always ask, "Is this worth arguing over?" If it is, can you work through the disagreement in a healthy way? Sometimes it's important to take some time to try to understand what the other person sees.

With this image, I'm not sure what the answer is, but at least I took the time to see it from a new perspective when I was given an alternate answer. I didn't argue that my answer was the right one. Honestly, this optical illusion isn't even worth arguing over.

The Bible reminds us to be careful with what we argue over. 2 Timothy 2:23 says, "*Again I say, don't get involved in foolish, ignorant arguments that only start fights*" (NLT).

Make sure that what you consider important is worth fighting over, and if you do choose to argue over something, don't be ignorant. Make sure you know what you're talking about. Consider other perspectives and don't be caught in a foolish argument.

---

7 "Impossible staircase," *Wikipedia*. May 19, 2005 (https://en.wikipedia.org/wiki/File:Impossible_staircase.svg).

8 The idea for this devotion was inspired by an object lesson about optical illusions from: *Sing & Play Roar and Safari Celebration Leader Manual* (Loveland, CO: Group Publishing, 2019), 21.

Art Challenge

M.C. Escher drew optical illusions, including ones with stairs that boggle the mind. If you're able, look up some of his work. Pick one or more optical illusions and practice sketching or creating them. Maybe you could make your own creative take on the Penrose Stairs pictured in this devotion."

Sharing Our Faith Story through Symbolism

READ MATTHEW 13:34–35, PSALM 78:1–2

> *Jesus spoke all these things to the crowd in parables; he did not say anything to them without using a parable.*
>
> —Matthew 13:34

Two years ago, I had surgery for a tachycardic heart rhythm. My heartrate sped up frequently, making it more difficult to do some basic tasks, and it often left me short of breath. I sometimes noticed it most while singing worship songs in church on Sunday mornings. My heartrate would increase as I stood, but even more so when I sang. So I often stood and only mouthed the words.

Following the surgery I experienced many changes, but one of the most profound moments was when I was able to praise God while singing in worship—because I actually could again! It brought me such joy to be able to sing with all my heart, and I'm continually grateful for this change in my life.

I wanted to paint about my journey, and God helped me envision it using a heart with all the valves. As I studied the valves, the valves that brought blood into the heart were the ones that represented my past. I curved them to the bottom left of the painting, and in that corner the valves had darker tones and red colouring. They transformed into wires, representing the tachycardic rhythm, which spread into disarray. Here the wires were surrounded by musical symbols and notes that symbolized discord, like sharps, flats, and rests.

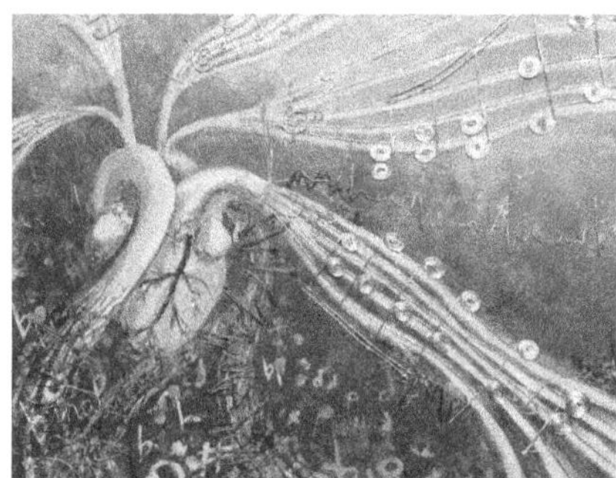

Then Sings My Soul
mixed media with acrylic and wire

On the right-hand side of the canvas were the valves known to bring circulation out of the heart, and they represented the present. I showed this in the upper right portion of the painting. Out of my heart flowed a healthy rhythm and lighter colours, but also an organized and beautiful song. If you're able to read music, you could play it; they are the notes of a familiar hymn and represent the words "Then sings my soul," which is also the title of the painting.[9]

---

9 Colour images of this artwork is available to view online: https://ktmmv6.wixsite.com/mysite/gallery, or on Facebook at: https://www.facebook.com/artisticworksoftinarae

Jesus used parables and metaphors in His teaching to illustrate a point and convey a better understanding to the teachings in the Bible. He told stories with images that brought clarity and explained concepts that were otherwise difficult to understand.

We can do the same thing through the art we create. When we draw or paint, we can take the story of our lives and bring clarity to aspects of it through images that explain that which can be difficult to articulate or understand—and we can even share our faith.

Art Challenge

Think of your personal story or a certain event that has happened in your life. What symbols, colours, words, or ideas come to mind that could help communicate the story to others? Write or draw them here or on a blank page.

Visio Divina

READ JOHN 3:1–8

The wind blows wherever it pleases. You hear its sound, but you cannot tell where it comes from or where it is going. So it is with everyone born of the Spirit.

—John 3:8

Sometimes there are moments in daily life when God brings an image to mind that impacts me in a particular way. I need to write it down or sketch it out, and I feel moved to create it into a piece of artwork to represent the thoughts I was thinking in that moment.

Recently, I was at a retreat and heard a talk from Shaila Visser, the National Director of Alpha Canada. She shared her testimony and the amazing story of how she wrestled with God.

Near the end of her talk she said, "I want to hold onto the coattails of the Holy Spirit and never let go." In that moment, I imagined someone holding onto a beautiful dove, because they wanted only to follow the leading of the Holy Spirit. I sketched it and wrote down the words that caught my attention.

As the idea continued to develop in my mind, I carefully considered the colouring I would use, the idea of spirituality I would represent, and the message I wanted to communicate. I used purples and golds to represent royalty. I decided not to illustrate a person holding onto the tailfeathers, because that seemed violent; instead I drew hands reaching for the Spirit in the background. I used metals to add a unique texture, but also to play with the light and make the painting come alive. I also shaped the wires into spirals to symbolize the Spirit and the wind.

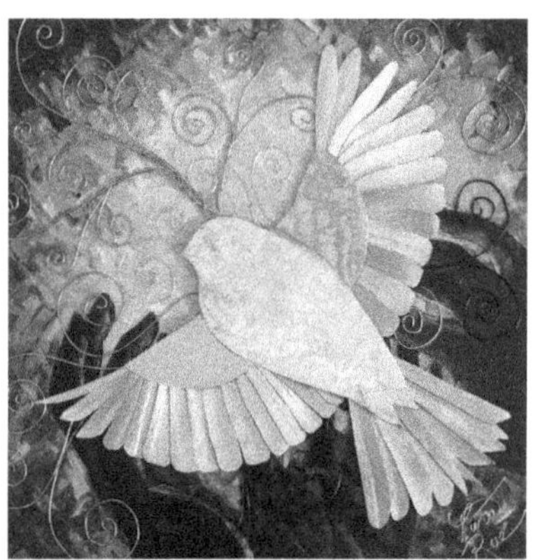

Leading
mixed media with aluminum, acrylic, and wire

I loved putting this piece together, even though it took a great deal of time and thought. It spoke to me and spoke to others. Some people saw and understood the symbolism, while others did not, but even these people were struck by the image without really being able to articulate why.

Sometimes we need to put what comes to our mind on paper or a canvas, because it helps others grasp and understand an idea. When the image of the dove came to mind, I could have only appreciated it for myself, but instead I chose to share it—and because I did, I have created meaning and value that many people have connected with.

Art Challenge

Is there an image on your mind that represents something significant God might be saying to you? If not, listen to a worship song or read through today's passage and look for a word or image that stands out to you. Take the image and start drawing it. See where the Holy Spirit leads as you create.

Beauty in Many Stages

READ ECCLESIASTES 3:1–11

He has made everything beautiful in its time.

—Ecclesiastes 3:11

I have Mondays off, so I often walk my children to school in the morning. In late fall, the evening dew had turned to frost overnight, outlining the edges of individual grass blades and the leaves that had begun to fall.

One morning, I thought the frost was so beautiful that I needed to capture it with my camera. So when I returned home, I grabbed the camera to take some images before the sun melted it away. Each image spoke to me, but some spoke to me more than others.

I took one image of a dying flower; it had browned edges and was missing petals. It was the kind of flower you often don't pay attention to because its life is over and the beauty is gone, but it caught my eye with the frost glinting in the morning sun. Despite its current insignificance, a moment of beauty still shone through.

We are all on a journey in our lives. We'll all have moments of beauty and joy, and moments of trials and sadness. But even in those difficult times, God can still bring us life and joy. So if you're experiencing a more difficult moment in your life, don't be discouraged. God can still make something beautiful in that moment.

Art Challenge

There are many stages in our lives. Is there a moment or transition that you have grown to appreciate more over time? I think about the sunflower series Van Gogh created where sunflowers are painted at many stages as they wilt. Draw something that is at a unique stage in its life and think about what makes it beautiful. Old or discarded items can have new life and beauty depending on how you look at them.

God Can Fix Broken Things

READ 1 KINGS 19:1–9

He heals the brokenhearted and binds up their wounds.

—Psalm 147:3

After a very busy day of painting faces, our family decided to go out for dinner with the money I'd earned. We had to park a short distance away from the restaurant, since we were downtown, and on our walk to the restaurant my eye caught several broken pieces of a mirror along the sidewalk. I immediately thought, *Those would be great to incorporate into my artwork.* I made a mental note to pick them up on our way back to the car before we headed home.

As we ate our meal, tiredness set upon me. I was shocked, because I wouldn't have thought painting faces would be so tiring. But the social interaction and my awkward position while painting had tired me out. I ended up feeling so tired that when I returned to the car, I passed the glass pieces, feeling that I didn't have the energy to collect them.

I went home and rested, but for days afterward I thought about how I wished that I had picked up those pieces. I had thought of a way to incorporate them into my art.

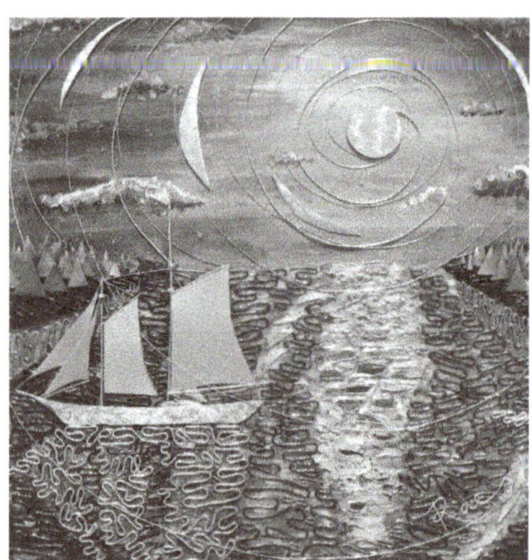

Moonlight Reflections
mixed media with aluminum, copper, acrylic, wire, and broken mirror pieces

Two weeks later, I was in the same area of downtown and running ahead of schedule. Wondering if the pieces were still there, I took the short walk to the area and discovered them still sitting on the sidewalk. Because the pieces were so small, the garbage pick-up had missed them. I collected the pieces, brought them home, and repurposed them in a mixed media piece I had created depicting the moon's reflection on a lake.

There are many moments when we feel broken, like those little pieces of mirror I found on the ground. You may feel hopeless, like nothing can be done to fix us.

In the Bible, Elijah felt so broken that he asked God to end his life. I'm not sure where you are at, or if you've ever felt that hopeless, but be encouraged that God still has a purpose for you. He can come into your broken life like he did for Elijah and bring comfort.

Finding those mirror pieces and repurposing them into my artwork was an artistic way to show that something that is broken can be taken, saved, and made new. Do you need healing today? Call out to God in prayer and invite Him to fix your brokenness.

Art Challenge

Find something that's broken and piece it together, giving it new life. You can also draw the broken item and reimagine it in its repaired state, or you can reimagine what it would look like if you repurposed it.

Painting Without Hands

READ PHILIPPIANS 4:10–14

…I have learned to be content whatever the circumstances.

—Philippians 4:11

Every year my grandma bought a new art calendar for her wall, and I always enjoyed looking through it. What made each calendar even more special was that they were always created to support artists who painted with their mouths or feet, because they were unable to paint using their hands.

As I flipped through the calendar, I often marvelled at the painting, especially the ones that were very realistic. I wondered how they had done such an amazing job. So many artists were represented who had either been born unable to use their hands or had experienced some sort of accident. All of them had overcome their limitations. They were filled with such a passion for art that the limits didn't hold them back. They found another way to express themselves artistically and share their passion.[10]

Many times in our lives, a limitation or obstacle seems to prevent us from achieving a goal. We read of many people in the Bible who also struggled through valid issues, such as being blind (Bartimaeus), unable to walk (John 5:3–9), too short (Zacchaeus), thrown in jail (Peter, John, Paul, Silas), or even depressed (Elijah). The Bible shows us how these people overcame their issues, and God was with them to help them overcome what had held them back.

In Philippians we read, *"I have learned to be content whatever the circumstances… I can do all this through him who gives me strength"* (Philippians 4:11, 13). God can help us through so many situations because He is able. Sometimes He will heal us or change the situation, but sometimes He'll help us work through it in a way we may never have even thought of.

Seek God in prayer today. Will you invite Him to work in your life to help you overcome a challenge you are currently facing?

---

10 If you want to check out some of the amazing artwork created by these artists, visit www.mfpacanada.com.

Art Challenge

Challenge yourself to create a drawing in a unique way. Use your non-dominant hand, or try using your feet or mouth to hold your pen or paintbrush. Try drawing something simple, perhaps something you have drawn in a previous devotion, or consider making an image to reflect the challenging situation you need to overcome.

Letting Your Light Shine

READ MATTHEW 5:14–16

> *In the same way, let your light shine before others, that they may see your good deeds and glorify your Father in heaven.*
>
> —Matthew 5:16

At our church, we have a talent night each year. It is intended to take the opportunity to share the gifts God has given to each of us. People have shared songs through singing or playing an instrument, shared jokes, recited Scripture, and done many other things from the stage. In addition to the performances, there has also been an area set aside for artists, knitters, woodworkers, quilters, and sculptors to share their talents.

I have often been blown away by the talent because I find that people either hide their talents or haven't had a place to share their gifts in the church. People can also be afraid to share what God has gifted them with because they think they aren't good enough or that they might be bragging.

God has given artists many gifts that can be used to worship Him, to share a story about our faith, to highlight the creation He has made, to share about a change in our lives, or to help us think differently about something. If we hide our gifts, how can we ever move someone to think about God in a new way, to worship Him, to build new relationships, or to contemplate the world He has created?

In Matthew 5, Jesus talks about hiding a light under a bowl and says that it's silly to hide a light like that, because hiding it makes it useless. He compares the useless light to a Christian who hides his or her faith. He says, *"In the same way [that we use a light to light a room], let your light shine before others, that they may see your good deeds and glorify your Father in heaven"* (Matthew 5:16).

Knowing and following Jesus isn't something we are meant to hide, just like we are not meant to hide lights under bowls or to hide our gifts and talents. You can still be humble about sharing your art, but many of us need a challenge to share our work, and I think our artwork can be, and is, a way to share our faith.

Consider whether you should take the time to share your talent with those around you. You never know how God could use your gifts to encourage someone, to speak to them in a unique way, or to begin a conversation about your faith. Share the gift God has given you for Him.

Art Challenge

Create a drawing or piece of artwork that says something about your faith, and then give it away. This is an opportunity to share your artwork. Depending on how comfortable you are with sharing your work, feel free to leave it where a stranger can find it without telling them who it's from. Alternatively, you could also give it to a close friend.

Noticing the Unnoticed

READ PSALM 104:24, 33–34

> *How many are your works, Lord! In wisdom you made them all; the earth is full of your creatures… I will sing to the Lord all my life; I will sing praise to my God as long as I live. May my meditation be pleasing to him, as I rejoice in the Lord.*
>
> —Psalm 104:24, 33–34

I once heard a story about a scientist who had an apprentice.[11] The scientist gave the apprentice one task: to study a fish. The apprentice was to record all his observations in a notebook, and when he was finished he was to report back to the scientist.

The apprentice spent an hour looking at the fish and then reported back. The apprentice had taken the time to draw it and created a diagram, labeling all the parts of the fish. Unfortunately, the scientist wasn't satisfied and sent him back to study the fish some more.

The apprentice was a bit surprised, because he had thought his work was quite satisfactory. But as he sat and looked closer, he noticed that there was, in fact, more to discover. Instead of only noting a fin, he noticed that there were bones that held the fins up and webbing in between. He added shading and colour into his diagram and noted more specific details.

At the end of the day, he turned in his work. The scientist noted that the work was much improved, but there was still more work to be done.

By this time, the apprentice had spent a whole day on the assignment and was upset that he had done so much work on such a meaningless task. He returned the next day quite frustrated, but having spent more time with the fish he was surprised at how much more he had taken note of. He had counted the scales and noted the number of bones, among other things.

By the end of the second day, he still didn't feel that he was done. There was more and more to discover.

As artists, we need to go deeper and notice the unnoticed—and bring attention to it. Just like the apprentice learned to appreciate the intricacies of the fish, we need to appreciate the world around us that God created. If we are realistic artists, we need to show all those details and be careful not to miss any. If we want to create emotion, we need to pay close attention to the lines, shapes, colours, and textures we use to evoke a similar emotion in our work.

---

11 This is a paraphrase of a story told in a high school science class.

We also need to see what the average person may miss, like the miniscule creations God has made, the tiny waterdrops, the insects, or the frost patterns on a window. Perhaps we need to paint or draw something in plain sight, something we usually just pass by, such as that flower growing between a crack in the sidewalk, the formation of clouds in the sky, or the way a child scrunches her face when she laughs.

Art Challenge

Art is inspired by capturing these moments and images and bringing them to life in our artwork. Take the time today to go on a walk and be curious. What has escaped your attention? Choose something you have seen on your walk, or even around your house, and sketch it here, noting all the details.

Value in Every Part

READ 1 CORINTHIANS 12:12–20

> *Just as a body, though one, has many parts, but all its many parts form one body, so it is with Christ.*
>
> —1 Corinthians 12:12

Growing up, I loved getting supplies for going back to school. I loved the newness of the supplies, but also the completeness of new sets. I particularly enjoyed getting a fresh set of pencil crayons. During the previous year, favourite or important colours would get used up and need to be replaced.

As an adult, I have the same appreciation and need for a complete set of colours, with my coloured pencils as well as my paints. Although I could live without some colours in my paint set, I do need to have all the primary colours—and I appreciate the secondary colours as well. The reason I need all these colours is that every colour is important, and it's difficult to complete a satisfactory painting without specific colours.

For a realistic painter, specific colours must be used for certain objects as you determine to match the colours of the world around you. For an abstract worker, you may seek to challenge how colour is used, but colour choice must still achieve balance and flow. In still other circumstances, only hues of one colour may be used, like if you were creating a monochrome painting—but you choose that one colour for a reason and use it to communicate an emotion or mood to the viewer.

Every colour is important.

In today's passage, we are given the same understanding: every part of the body of Christ is important, just as we know that every colour in the palette is important. The body of Christ has many parts and people with many gifts and talents, and all are important for sharing the message of Christ and building one another up. In the same way, every colour in your set serves a purpose.

Art Challenge

Create something that uses all the colours of the rainbow or focus on the importance of one colour in a monochromatic piece of artwork. If you choose the second option, decide which colour you want to use and then use varying shades of that colour to create the finer details. Take time to think about why you are using that colour. What emotion are you trying to convey? Which colour highlights the mood of happiness, joy, sadness, royalty, or whatever theme you want to highlight? Use black and white to tint your colours if you choose to use paint.

Revisiting Our Source

READ COLOSSIANS 1:15–18

He is before all things, and in him all things hold together.

—Colossians 1:17

When I was a child, my mom would organize birthday parties at our house. We would be allowed to invite a certain number of friends and play games together. Mom was the party planner and prepared all kinds of games for us, including prizes.

One of the games I enjoyed most was one where we had to be blindfolded and draw a picture. My mom would announce an image to draw and count down so that we began together. We then proceeded to draw for an allotted period of time. At the end, we all looked and assessed our work.

I struggled the first time I played, because I really didn't like my picture. It looked terrible, in fact! It was a relief to me that my friends' pictures weren't much better. The eyes weren't level, the noses weren't even on the face, and often the face wasn't even a complete circle.

I didn't want to accept defeat, because I just knew I could do better. I practiced on my own for future parties, and over time I learned that if I kept one finger in one place on the page and remembered what I had drawn there, my pictures improved exponentially. Once I finished drawing one part of the image, I would know approximately how far the next feature should be from the starting point. The images still weren't perfect, of course, since I was still drawing with my eyes closed, but at least the image resembled the object I was trying to draw.

The key is to start with an anchor. Similarly, I am reminded that I need to frequently come back to Jesus when I need some direction. Jesus is our anchor, and He is always there for us. As we travel through life, we may feel lost or uncertain about where we are going, but if we place our trust in Jesus we can always come back to Him, get reoriented, and continue on the next steps in our journey.

Art Challenge

Try drawing a couple of pictures with your eyes closed. Attempt one where you don't have a marked starting point, and then a second one where you mark the starting point with a finger on your non-dominant hand. Some drawing ideas could include a face, a pig, or a cat.

Three in One

READ JOHN 14:9–11, EPHESIANS 4:4–6, JOHN 1:14

> *For there are three that testify: the Spirit, the water and the blood; and the three are in agreement.*
>
> —1 John 5:7–8

I have worked for many years in children's ministries, and one of my favourite ways to help kids understand an issue is through object lessons. Jesus often used objects or relatable stories to help bring clarity to an issue. Jesus called Himself *"the bread of life"* (John 6:35), *"the light of the world"* (John 8:12), *"the gate"* (John 10:9), *"the good shepherd"* (John 10:11), and *"the vine"* (John 15:5). He used these comparisons to help people better understand who He was.

Over the years, many people have used objects to help others better understand Christ. One of those people was Saint Patrick, whom many Irish people know well. Saint Patrick delighted in finding everyday objects around him to bring clarity to the people he wanted to share his faith with.

One of his most famous object lessons used the shamrock to illustrate the Trinity, which is the idea that God the Father, God the Son, and God the Holy Spirit are all one yet distinct in some ways. When he used the shamrock, he was able to show that there were three separate leaves, yet they all came together and joined into one stem.

In the artist's world, there is another way in which we can illustrate this concept: by considering how we blend colours together. There are three primary colours that are distinct from one another, but you can blend these colours with one another to create some overlap.

With both the examples of the shamrock and primary colours, we can see that there is a distinct difference between the three, yet also a place where they overlap and come together. When considering God the Father, God the Son, and God the Holy Spirit, we see overlap when Jesus says that He and the Father are one (John 10:30), that He will leave the Spirit in His place when He is risen (John 7:38–39), and when God is described as the Spirit (Genesis 1:2). All three connect to one another and are one and the same in many ways.

Art Challenge

Fill the circles with coloured line art or patterns, making sure to use one colour of varying shades per section. The main circles would be red, yellow, and blue, with the overlapping sections filled with the secondary colours created when you mix the primary colours. For example, red and yellow would make orange. In the very centre, where all three colours connect, mixing all the colours will create black, so use varying shades of black and gray.

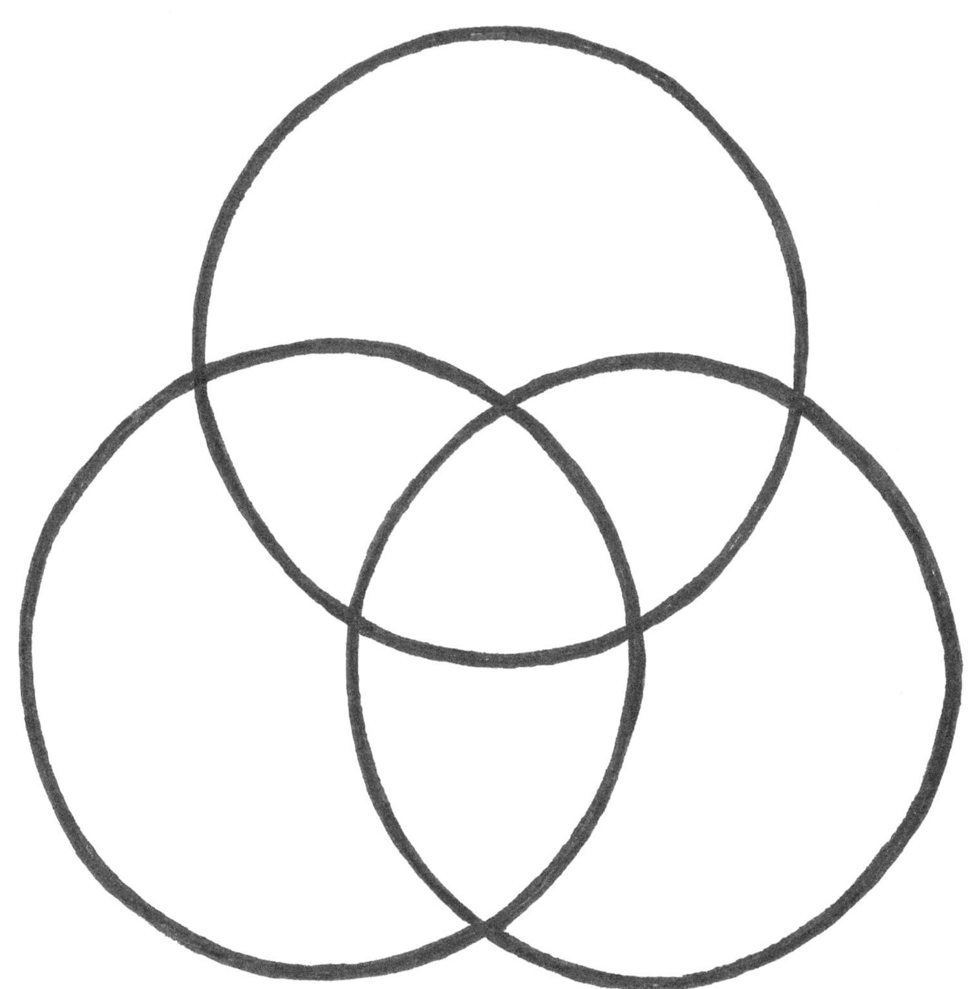

Dream Big, but Start Small

READ MARK 4:30–34

> *It is like a mustard seed, which is the smallest of all seeds on earth. Yet when planted, it grows and becomes the largest of all garden plants…*
>
> —Mark 4:31–32

When we're young, we want to be formidable when we grow up. We want to be the richest, the smartest, the fastest, the most successful. As adults, we may still have such big dreams, and if we're creative in any way we may also apply these dreams to our artistic goals. We may want to paint the perfect painting, or have a creative idea nobody else has had, or have huge sales, or become famous for our work, etc.

The problem can be that sometimes we dream so big that in the next moment we consider the cost, time, effort, and practice needed—and get discouraged. Sometimes we give up.

Amidst our big dreams, we need to remember to start small and just get started. We may need to be intentional about setting aside time to paint, to carry a sketchbook, or to sign up for an art class. These are small art goals, but they can be faith goals as well.

I have felt that it's important to bridge faith and art, because I believe we can worship God through our art. I've felt that calling but haven't exactly known how to do it. The goal seemed big, but in obedience I moved forward as best I could to see what would develop.

I've had thoughts that have discouraged me—*I can't do this, I don't know exactly what God wants me to do*—but I've started small. I started by teaching art classes with our youth group and local art centre, by sketching when my kids were at lessons, by actually taking the step to share my art online, and by entering my art in a local fair. These steps are just the beginning of growing confidence in our art, but also in opening doors to share our faith.

I feel that the dream God has for me is just beginning, and I know that God has faithfully been encouraging me along the way. When I faithfully take these small steps forward, I feel God's affirmation, and I know He can grow something big from that.

Art Challenge

Have you had a big dream in mind and haven't known where to start? What is a smaller and more achievable goal that can help you get started in the right direction? It may or may not be art-related. Jot down that small idea inside the shape of a small seed, then draw a plant or tree that could grow from it to help you move forward. Let God grow it.

The Comparison Trap

READ GALATIANS 6:1–6

> *Each one should test their own actions. Then they can take pride in themselves alone, without comparing themselves to someone else…*
>
> —Galatians 6:4

You may have heard the expression that says the grass is always greener on the other side of the fence. In other words, when we compare what we have to what our neighbour has, it often seems as though they are better off than we are.

Unfortunately, we easily fall into this trap. I grew up being what some people might call an overachiever; I wanted to earn the best marks, to do the best work, and win all the awards. I often found myself comparing my work to others and felt that what I created wasn't as good as theirs. I thought my story wasn't as good, or that my artwork needed something more. In other situations, I unrealistically compared myself to someone who was older or had more experience, setting myself up for personal failure.

To learn a technique, you often need to have a reference to which you can compare your work, but you need to keep that purpose in mind. If you're aiming for perfection, you often lose out.

I still struggle with comparison, and to remind myself of this pitfall I've placed a quote on my desk. Teddy Roosevelt once said, "Comparison is the thief of joy." This quote is there to remind me every day that comparing myself to others can be dangerous.

Some of us are called to share our art with others to bring glory to God, and some of us are called to worship God independently with our art. With this devotional, don't feel that you need to show or compare the artwork you create here. If you feel led to share your artwork, do it for God and be careful not to fall into the trap of comparison. If drawing out your ideas and communicating with God through sketching gives you clarity of thought and helps you connect with God, don't share your work.

Whatever you do, be careful not to lose your joy in the process of creating something beautiful for God.

Art Challenge

Use the divided page and consider what you might be comparing yourself or your work to. On one side of the page, draw or write who you are in Christ and consider what God has called you to do. Make sure you use bright and cheerful colours to reflect the joy God has in who He has called you to be. On the other side, consider the negative outcomes of comparing yourself to someone else. Use dark colours that communicate the sadness and anger that may result from the joy that's lost when you compare yourself to others.

Who am I in Christ?	Comparison Traps

The Big Picture

READ PROVERBS 3:5–6

> *Trust in the Lord with all your heart and lean not on your own understanding; in all your ways submit to him, and he will make your paths straight.*
>
> —Proverbs 3:5–6

When I was younger, I enjoyed putting puzzles together. Getting all those pieces in the right place was so satisfying. I loved puzzles so much that my mom thought she would challenge me by getting me a seemingly impossible puzzle with 500 pieces where almost all the pieces looked the same. The box only showed part of the picture, there was no edge, and there were five extra pieces. That sure was a challenge!

Although I loved puzzles, this one never got finished. I finished the part that had been pictured on the front of the box, but left the repetitive and overlapping flowers surrounding it. I didn't know the whole picture, where the edges were, and I got frustrated with testing every single puzzle edge to see if it fit.

The box was sealed when I got it, so I knew everything was there and that it could be completed. But I lacked patience and perseverance. I also wanted to see the whole picture on the box to know where the edges were and when I was getting close to the end.

Sometimes we can get impatient with what's happening in our lives. We ask questions like, where is God taking me? What will happen next? When will I get through this difficult period? The questions can go on and on. We can be frustrated because we only see a small part of our lives and don't know the future.

In times of uncertainty, I'm thankful that our God knows the big picture. He knows the plans He has for us, but He also knows the plans He has for all of His followers, for the nations, and for all people who will ever live on this earth.

I pray that God's plans for my life are good, but even when they seem difficult I have faith that God has a reason why I am in such a season of my life. God will see me through it, because He has a good plan. We should daily remind ourselves to place our trust in Him, for He will show us through our difficulties with His knowledge and understanding.

Art Challenge

Create a drawing where you can only see a piece of the subject. You can zoom in and pay close attention to that small section or draw a large object and draw it to scale, but only include a portion that can fit on the page you're drawing on. If you want to add an extra challenge, ask someone if they can figure out what the big picture would be if you drew the whole picture.

Group Challenge: Work on a large piece of artwork that is outlined but not coloured, and then cut it into several pieces for your group. Have each person colour one section. When each person is finished, bring all the pieces back together to recreate the larger picture.

Prayer through Your Art

READ 1 TIMOTHY 2:1–6

> *I urge, then, first of all, that petitions, prayers, intercession and thanksgiving be made for all people…*
>
> —1 Timothy 2:1

I first heard of Elizabeth Londen in a Facebook group for Christian Artists I joined. She had posted a request for pictures of butterflies, both as photographs or images of artwork. I had a few, so I sent them her way. After that, we connected and I quietly watched her posts come through my Facebook feed.

I learned that she started her website, Art on a Mission, after having this contemplation: "how as a young person, who has nothing but a heart on fire for God and the gift of art, how can I make a difference? How can I serve Him well? What will impact the community? How can I inspire others to do the same? Is it even possible?"[12]

In the process of sifting through this calling, she started painting murals in St. Louis, giving up a week per month to brighten the walls of her community as she glorifies God. She has wholly given this work to God and placed it in His hands.

Elizabeth has had some uncertain moments while preparing for the butterfly mural, but God has provided the right people and the right place. As a result of prayer and God's leading, she will be painting her butterfly mural on the walls of a homeless shelter for single pregnant women and their children.

I was amazed to see her posts asking for people to pray for the women and families who spend time in this facility. She has asked for more than that moment spent between you and God, that moment when we trust that all prayers have been prayed; she has asked for prayers to be written down so she can later transcribe them onto the walls of the mural.

She wrote 104 prayers for this particular mural, and now that she's taken the time to transcribe the prayers, they will be painted over. I will not be able to read these prayers, but that's okay because the point is not for them to be read; the point is for this mural, this place in her community, to be literally covered in prayer. The artist's intention is that God's presence is, and always will be, a part of this place.

---

12 Elizabeth Londen, "Art on A Mission," *Patreon.* Date of access: September 9, 2019 (https://www.patreon.com/ArtonaMission).

Art Challenge

Think of a place in your community that needs prayer. What would your prayer be? Plan to write out that prayer. If you're using paper, incorporate the prayer in and around a drawing that represents the hope you have for your community. If you have access to a canvas, write out your words and then cover them up, just as Elizabeth did. Paint an image of the organization's building, an image of hope, praying hands, or paint as you feel God's leading.

Seasons of Change

READ 2 CORINTHIANS 4:1–6

> *For God, who said, "Let light shine out of darkness," made his light shine in our hearts to give us the light of the knowledge of God's glory displayed in the face of Christ.*
>
> —2 Corinthians 4:6

My favourite season is spring. It's not too hot and not too cold, and it's a season of growth and change when the dark, dreary, and cold days slowly evolve into brighter and warmer days filled with new life and colour.

I've often wished that it was spring all the time, since I dislike the scorching summers and freezing winters, but without these extremes I might not appreciate spring as much as I do. If it was always spring, I likely wouldn't appreciate the beauty, because it would become routine or boring.

God challenges us to think about our everyday lives and about how much better our lives can be with Him. The Bible uses contrasting terms to help us see and understand that there is such a big difference between how our lives were before we knew Christ and how our lives are after. We need to know that there is darkness in our sin, but we need to see and understand that there is something better in Christ. We can be changed people when we understand that.

If you've accepted Christ into your life, consider the importance of sharing your whole story of changing from the dark days without Christ to the glorious ones you've experienced with God in your life. Sometimes we only highlight the positive, and although I praise God for the positive others need to see the contrast in how I have changed and become who I am.

Therefore, when you find a person who needs to hear your story, make sure you share the whole story and don't gloss over the struggles you have faced. Our flaws make it easier for people to relate to us, to know that they can change as well.

Prayerfully consider who needs to hear your story and let them see how your life has changed and brought you from darkness into the light.

Art Challenge

Look around and choose an object to draw. When drawing it, pay attention to the shadows in your artwork. As you think about how important sharing the difficult parts in your life may be, consider how the object would look without shadows. Creating artwork without shadows can make the artwork look unrealistic, and it may lack definition. Take time to see the value in how the shadows bring definition to the object, just as those moments in your life can help highlight who you are today.

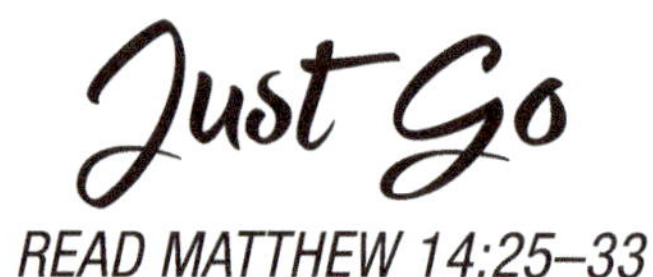

Just Go

READ MATTHEW 14:25–33

But Jesus immediately said to them: "Take courage! It is I. Don't be afraid."

—Matthew 14:27

Have you ever sat in front of a blank page, unable to think of what you should write, paint, or create? A couple of days ago when I was on vacation, I told my kids that we would work on art pieces for our town's upcoming fair. We all decided to work on entries for the painting and drawing contests. My children got straight into what they wanted to paint while I, unfortunately, didn't put a single stroke on my page.

I knew I wanted to paint a still life, or a person, but I had set so many parameters on myself. I knew I wanted it to be original, but it needed to be realistic, so I needed an image to look at. I started looking through my photographs, filled with excuses. My photos were too complicated, too much work, not the right composition, the wrong lighting, not quite the subject I was looking to paint, not appealing enough to win a category in the fair, etc. While my children completed their artwork, I hadn't even begun.

Sometimes we overcomplicate the creative process. We can be our own worst enemies, working against ourselves, like the many disciples who couldn't even get out of the boat to meet Jesus. Amazingly, Peter did get out of the boat. He was afraid, but he didn't let fears or excuses get in the way. With his eyes on Jesus, he was able to do the impossible. He even doubted himself when he was already in the water, but Jesus helped him amid his turbulent steps while he miraculously walked on the water toward Him.

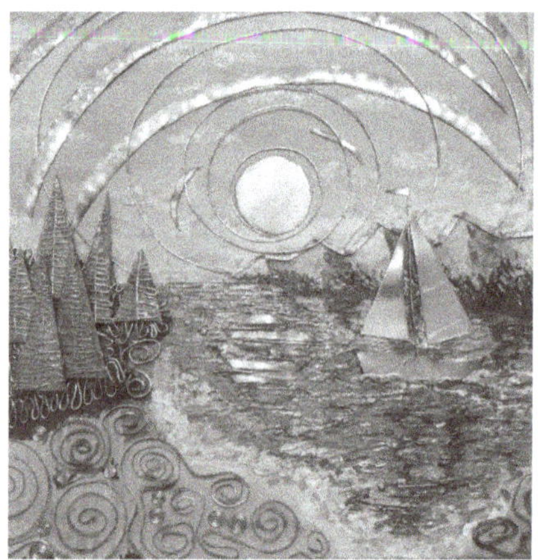

My first painting sold in a gallery.
Lakeside Sunset
mixed media with acrylic, copper, and wire

We need to remember that whatever we do, we need to always step forward and do it for Him.

In contrast to the stories of painters' block, I also have stories of times when I took a step forward. In fact, that was how I got into mixed media, working with metals. My husband suggested that I make something from his leftover copper, and over the next few months I put a piece of artwork together which ended up being my first painting that I sold in a gallery.

So pull out the paints, the pencils, the mixed media, and just get started. You never know what may form from the first few strokes you put on the page. It will be so much better to get painting and get the creative juices flowing than to feel disappointed and have nothing to show for the time you've set aside to create.

Art Challenge

Use the beginning of the drawing on this page or draw some random shapes of your own. What could those shapes be part of? Continue the drawing and see what creative ideas you come up with. Try this challenge in a group and see how many different ideas you have.

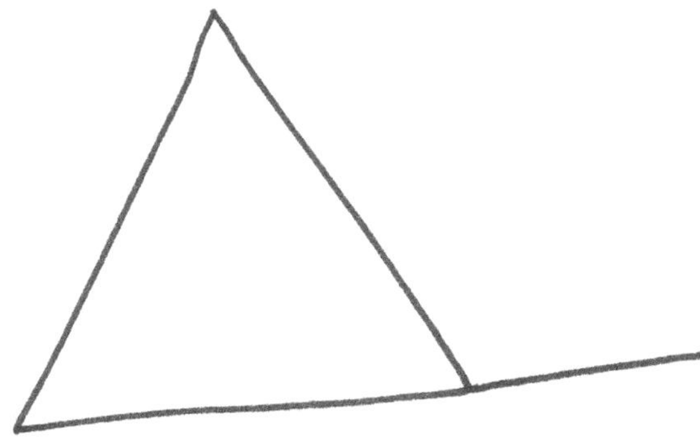

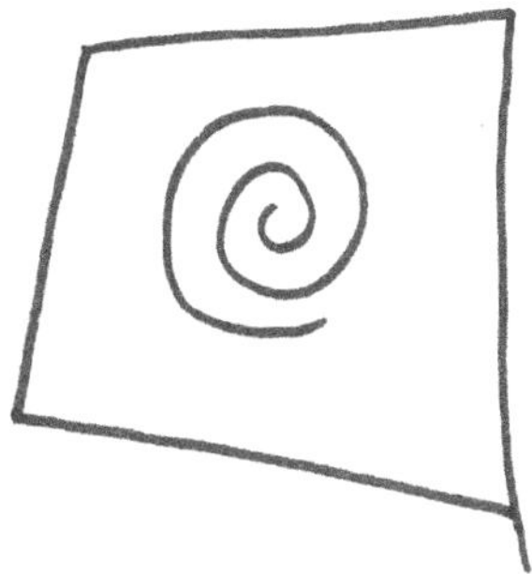

Waiting on God's Leading

READ PSALM 32

I will instruct you and teach you in the way you should go; I will counsel you with my loving eye on you.

—Psalm 32:8

Many times in my life, I have felt lost. I have come to God and asked, "Where do you want me to go? What do you want me to do?" I've prayed and felt just as lost when I was finished. I still didn't know where to go or what to do.

When I'm in one of these situations, I need to think back on times when God has been clear to me. Although I cannot say that I've personally heard an audible message from God, I have at times been certain that my own thoughts could only have come from God.

One of these times has come through developing this book. A year and a half ago, I was certain that I had heard from God, but the message didn't seem so clear to me.

I had been asked to design the stage for our Baptist women's conference, and I loved how everything came together. As we praised God through song at the conference, I had a moment when my breath was taken away. I've learned that it's important to pay attention to moments like these, so I wrote down what was on my mind. I felt God clearly say, "You help others worship God through art." I wrote it down so I wouldn't forget, so that I could be continually encouraged.

But I didn't know exactly what it meant.

I have taken steps forward, unsure about what to do with that, but God continued to affirm my journey. Although more than a year passed before I started writing this book, I proceeded slowly, still not knowing if it was the right thing to do.

At a more recent conference, I shared my artistic calling with a pastor I had never met. I told her that I was unsure about how to bridge faith and art, and I asked for clarity as she prayed for me. I hadn't told her that I was starting to write a book, so I was shocked when she prayed that God would help me bridge art and faith… through a devotional or short book.

I waited until we finished praying, and then shared with her how encouraging her prayer had been—that she would pray about this book without having known a thing about it! It was another affirmation from God that I was on the right track.

I needed to take a step forward, to move faithfully, even though I didn't know exactly what God meant. I felt affirmed along the way, and I'm thankful that God is walking alongside me with this.

Where might God be prompting you in your journey? Has He revealed a passion in your life, shown you an important person, renewed your faith, or resparked joy in something for which you once had little joy? Plan to take a step forward in giving that area of your life to God by pursuing it, praying about it, and asking for God's affirmation.

Art Challenge

As an artistic response, draw a symbol or image that represents the area of your life that came to mind at the end of this devotion. Add artistic design, words, and colour to reflect what this idea means to you. Draw out how you think God may want you to take some first steps in fulfilling this dream.

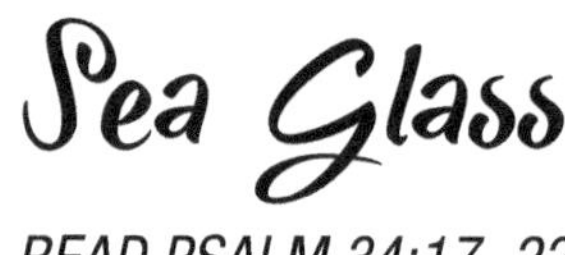

READ PSALM 34:17–22

The Lord is close to the brokenhearted and saves those who are crushed in spirit.

—Psalm 34:18

Whenever I find myself at a beach, I love to look for little treasures. One of the treasures I look for is sea glass, which is glass that's been broken somewhere by the shore so that over time the water and waves continue to wash over it, wearing down the sharp edges until they're no longer sharp.[13]

This reminds me of some of the tough days in my life, when difficult events have happened. Some days I can feel like broken glass.

Depending on how big the event is, you can hurt for a little while or you can hurt for a long time, but God is with you and will help you through these tough times. He can bring people alongside you to give you words of encouragement, to listen to you, to give you hugs, and to wipe away your tears. One word or moment of encouragement may not be enough, but over time the many ways in which you are comforted bring healing.

Psalm 34:18 says, *"The Lord is close to the brokenhearted and saves those who are crushed in spirit."* When God and those around you bring you comfort, it will help you feel a little better each day so that the parts of you that feel broken will hurt less and less. And over time, just like the waves moved along the sharp edges of the sea glass and smoothed them down, your hurt can be lessened too.

Today I want to encourage you that God can comfort you, heal you, and make you beautiful, even after those difficult days.

---

13 The idea for this devotion was inspired by an object lesson about sea glass from: *Sing & Play and Sail Away Sendoff Leader Manual* (Loveland, CO: Group Publishing, 2018), 49–50.

Art Challenge

If you are able, go for a walk on a local beach to find some sea glass or a smoothed stone. If you cannot get to a beach, draw a beach scene. As you're drawing or going for your walk, consider how God may have smoothed the rough edges in your life to help you work through a difficult period of time. If you do find sea glass or a rock, make it into something creative.

A New Vision

READ ACTS 26:4–18

Immediately, something like scales fell from Saul's eyes, and he could see again.

—Acts 9:18

One great new invention that has really intrigued me is colour blindness glasses. Several men and one female friend of mine are colour blind and see the world differently than I do. If you look this up online, you can find examples of the differences between how those with colour blindness may see the world and those of us who perceive the full colour spectrum.

Because of the invention of colour blindness glasses, those who are colour blind are now able to see the difference. I've seen several heartwarming videos of individuals who have received their first pair of glasses that enable them to see colour.

Often they are timid to try them on, but they're surrounded by encouraging friends or family. Everyone around the person knows that this will be a significant event, so they film it and prepare with balloons or other coloured items to help show the before-and-after difference.

The moment these people put on the glasses and take in the world, they are filled with wonder and tears of joy to see the beauty they have been missing all these years—and perhaps they also have a few tears of sadness.

Paul had a similar moment in Acts. Paul saw the world one way; it was a dark way that involved hurting and killing those who believed in Christ. Thankfully, God met him one day and gave him a new way to see the world. Acts 9:18 says that *"something like scales fell from Saul's eyes"* and he was able to see. He was physically blind and then able to see, but he was also spiritually blind and then able to see—and it changed him.

Is there something you have seen in a new way? It may be coming to know Christ, caring more for the world around you, or forgiving a person you couldn't forgive before. How have you started to see things differently?

Art Challenge

Create an image that shows the change in how you now see things differently. The page has already been divided into two areas where you can show the differences between before and after.

Before	After

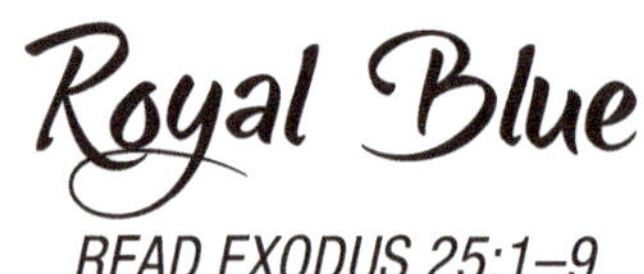

READ EXODUS 25:1–9

These are the offerings you are to receive from them: gold, silver and bronze; blue, purple and scarlet yarn and fine linen...

—Exodus 25:3–4

I grew up loving almost everything Dutch, because my grandparents on both sides of my family were born in the Netherlands before they moved to Canada. As we reminisced and taught about our heritage, I heard stories, was shown pictures, and got to experience parts of our historic culture. I loved all of it—the food, the stories, the Dutch shoes, and the Dutch art, including the Dutch pottery, which is famous for being white and blue in colour.

Since I loved all things Dutch, I attributed this style solely to the Netherlands, but I have learned that this artistic style has a history that goes back even further. The Dutch were inspired by the Chinese, who had already created pottery with the beautiful blue colour. However, the pottery was quite expensive, so they creatively found another way to make it with a tin glaze which turned blue when fired.[14]

Throughout the ages, both blue and purple have been highly valued because they were such rare colours. They were known as the colours for royalty and the rich, because only they could afford them.

When the tabernacle was built, God required these valuable colours to be woven into the fabrics because they were fit for a place to worship Him (Exodus 25–28, 35–36, 38–39). Later on, blue was also incorporated into the temple when Solomon had it built (2 Chronicles 2). Blue was so valuable that one source says blue cobalt was once considered to be twice as valuable as gold.[15]

Blue doesn't have the same value or meaning today that it did many years ago, as it has become more common and attainable. But it still holds many meanings. When evoking emotion in artwork, it is often associated with sadness, but it can also have connections to places like the Netherlands or China for their pottery. And it may still refer to royalty for some.

What does blue mean to you? Is it still a colour fit for our God and King?

---

14 Mina Solanki, "A Brief History of Delft Blue a.k.a Delfts Blauw," *I Am Expact.* November 10, 2017 (https://www.iamexpat.nl/lifestyle/lifestyle-news/brief-history-delft-blue-aka-delfts-blauw).

15 "Blue and White Pottery," *Wikipedia*. Date of access: September 15, 2019 (https://en.wikipedia.org/wiki/Blue_and_white_pottery).

Art Challenge

Create a piece of artwork using only shades of blue. Use the colour in the way that is most meaningful to you.

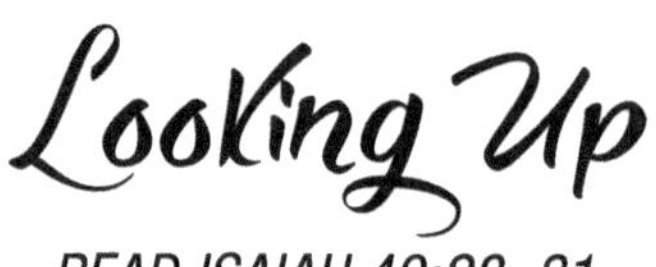

Looking Up

READ ISAIAH 40:28–31

> *But those who trust in the Lord will find new strength. They will soar high on wings like eagles. They will run and not grow weary. They will walk and not faint.*
>
> —Isaiah 40:31, NLT

Growing up in the country and being surrounded by farmers' fields, I repeatedly saw some very rewarding sights in the sky. Among my favourites were the hot air balloons that flew over our house and often landed in the nearby fields.

During the local balloon festival, I would see so many colours, designs, and even some unique shapes. I remember seeing a Canadian flag balloon, a pop can balloon, and even one shaped like a dinosaur. Although we loved seeing the special balloons, all balloons excited us, and if we noticed them soon enough we would jump on our bikes and chase them down, watching the landing with excitement.

We were wowed by the experience every time and were always disappointed if we learned that someone else noticed a balloon that we hadn't.

When we think about our faith, it's especially important to look beyond what is right in front of us and look up to God. He has so much to share with us, but if we aren't looking for Him and we aren't looking up, we may be disappointed and miss out. We need to look beyond the normal and mundane world. We need to believe in and trust in a God who will do the impossible, who will lead and guide us, and who will comfort us.

In today's passage, we read about our God who cares so much about us that we get a picture of how He will not only comfort us but also bring us to a place where we will *"soar high on wings like eagles."* When we look to God, we will be given strength and cared for in ways beyond what we may be able to imagine.

We need to take the time to look in new directions, both in our everyday lives and in our relationship with God. We need to come to God in prayer and ask for His leading and comfort.

Art Challenge

Draw something from the perspective of an observer looking up at it. What do the trees look like from directly below? Or buildings? Or the clouds? What would you look like to a toddler looking up at you? What do you see in the sky? If you need to, lay on the ground to get a new perspective and sketch what you see, and remember as you work through this activity that we should always be looking up to, and praising, our God and King.

Beautiful Words

READ EPHESIANS 4:25–29

> *Do not let any unwholesome talk come out of your mouths, but only what is helpful for building others up according to their needs, that it may benefit those who listen.*
>
> —Ephesians 4:29

If you go for a walk downtown in almost any city, it won't take long before you find some graffiti. The tag often stands out on a formerly pristine wall. Someone has taken it upon themselves to express themselves by placing a name or symbol to show they were there, or maybe they've written a curse word or statement to reflect their opinions.

People have a need to be creative and express themselves, but it's unfortunate that property is destroyed in the process of writing graffiti, and that such negative and hurtful words are shared through art.

Thankfully, there are people in our city who take it upon themselves to do a better job. I am thankful for the beautiful murals which beautify an otherwise plain space, but there are also walls of graffiti that are commissioned to make the area beautiful. It is wonderful to see the talents of artists used in a more positive manner.

One local graffiti artist was hired at our church to paint his work on the walls of our youth room. He realized his skill and found a positive outlet for his creativity. He painted Jesus on the cross with one word on either side, reading "Jesus Saves." Richard Phillips only paints his graffiti on walls when he is given permission and he shares the Gospel message in his work.[16]

Our words are very important, and we should be careful how we use them. In a moment, thoughtless or malicious words can really hurt someone. Writing words on a wall can be a visual reminder of how much more permanent they can be in our hearts.

However you speak or share your words, make sure that you carefully consider how they affect others. Are you building people up, being kind, and encouraging, or are you being hurtful, unkind, or tearing people down? Whatever you speak, be wise with your words.

---

16 "Christian Graffiti Artist Uses Medium to Spread Gospel Message," *The Underground*. September 22, 2010 (http://theundergroundsite.com/christian-graffiti-artist-uses-medium-to-spread-gospel/).

Art Challenge

Choose a word that reflects how God sees others. What would be a good word of encouragement? Write that word and embellish the letters with line patterns. Add more affirming words that support what God says about those He loves.

The Strength of Many

READ GENESIS 15:1–5, GENESIS 22:17, ECCLESIASTES 4:12

> *I will surely bless you and make your descendants as numerous as the stars in the sky and as the sand on the seashore.*
>
> —Genesis 22:17

Have you ever looked closely at a comic or newspaper photo? When you look closely, you'll notice the image is made up of many little dots. If it's a colour photo, you often see the primary colours overlapping or being placed close to one another so they appear to blend together when you look at the image from a normal distance.

Artwork that is created from dots like these is called pointillism. Up close, it's difficult to understand what the image is. All you see are dots. But from far away, the proper placement of the dots come together to make something beautiful.

If you think about it, you need a lot of dots and a lot of patience to create an image.

In the Old Testament, Abraham was told that he would be a father of many, as many as the stars in the sky, or even the grains of sand on the beach. Those are items that seem tiny from our perspective, but when added together they paint a powerful picture. It may have seemed like an unimaginable number to Abraham, because he was looking at his situation from up close. He had no sons and was quite old. He couldn't even imagine how he could be a father of many descendants.

Eventually, even at a very old age, God worked a miracle and gave Abraham the heir He had promised. With only one legitimate heir, Abraham may still have found it difficult to believe he would be a father of many generations, but as we read through the Bible we see that many sons and daughters were born in the generations that followed, just as God promised.

God can take something that is small and bring it together to make a big impact. It could be the vastness of the number of stars, the many grains of sand that fill a beach, or the number of descendants born to Abraham.

Maybe there have been times when you've felt small, insignificant, and alone, unable to achieve a big or grand plan. However, God can do great things with you when He brings you together with others. God can bring many people together to create community, to accomplish miracles, to help you to support one another, or to do more than you could imagine on your own.

Art Challenge

Create a piece of artwork using pointillism. To keep it simple, use only one colour. Vary the distance between the dots to create the illusion of shading. Dots that are closer together create dark shadows and those that are further apart imply a brighter surface. As you create your image, think about the many dots being used to create your picture, just as God can bring many details together to accomplish great things through you.

God Can Use Even Me

READ JONAH 1

But Jonah ran away from the Lord and headed for Tarshish.

—Jonah 1:3

I remember attending a youth service when I was a teen and learning about an art contest that caught my attention. For this art contest, we were to design a simple logo for a local drop-in centre. Ideas immediately came to mind and I was excited to enter.

However, there were a few rules: we were to design it with a friend, and that person had to come to the next service in a month, to find out who had won.

Those rules made things a little difficult for me, since I already had the idea. I did see the value of involving a friend and taking them to the service, especially for those who might need to know more about our faith. I decided to invite my second oldest sister. She seemed like the right person to ask.

The first thing I did when I got home was draw the whole logo and chose the colours I wanted. Then I approached my sister and explained the rules: "I need some help, and I need you to come with me to the next event." She agreed, so I gave her the logo along with the yellow and blue marker. I asked her to colour it in, and even told her where to put the colours. It was a very one-sided partnership.

She coloured it in, we sent it away, and then attended the next planned youth service.

I was so hopeful we would win. I knew that I may have had some self-centred motives along the way, but I had found a way to follow the rules and I felt good about the possible outcome.

However, God had some other plans that day.

They waited until the end to announce the winner, so we began the service with some games and worship music. During the worship, my sister left and went to the back of the sanctuary. I didn't know why she left, so I followed her and found her to be quite upset. I asked about what had happened and she had trouble explaining, but something had really impacted her. Unfortunately, she wanted to leave. I tried everything I could to get her to stay, because I really wanted to know who had won the contest, but as I said, God had other plans.

As we drove home, I learned that she had felt God's comfort in a tangible way, something she had never felt before. She had been overwhelmed by the knowledge of God's personal and unconditional love for her. She knew God was there, and God was real. This moment changed her life in a way I could never have planned on my own.

Sometimes we can get in the way of God's work, but God finds ways to break through even the most imperfect people and situations to accomplish His work. He can take Jonah, who went the opposite direction God had sent him, or Peter, who denied Him three times. Or He can take an imperfect person like me who is so self-absorbed in winning a contest to help change someone's life for Him.

Art Challenge

For today's challenge, heavily colour the page. Use lots of colourful crayons in no specific pattern. When you've finished, cover it all up with black crayon. Make sure you press heavily so that the colour below doesn't show through. Then take a coin or your fingernail and scratch a word or an image into the blackened area. You will find that the colour shows through vibrantly. This reminds me that God can work through any barrier. He can make His good work shine through.

Joyful Expressions

READ GENESIS 21:1–7

A cheerful heart is good medicine…

—Proverbs 17:22

When we get together a large enough gathering of people, one of the games our family loves to play is Telestrations.[17] For this game, good drawing skills come in handy, but the humour comes from people's bad drawing skills.

It's a lot like a game you may remember, called "Telephone," where a message is whispered from one person to the next until it reaches the last person. The last person then repeats what they thought the message was—and often it's not the same as what the first person said. Telestrations is very similar, except that it involves drawing.

In the game, someone draws the first image and passes it to the second person, who has to guess what has been drawn. The third person then has to draw the second person's guess, and the fourth person guesses what the third person's image shows. This continues until all eight people have guessed and drawn images. The final guess is often not the same as what was originally intended!

Lots of lessons can be learned from a game like this, but there is a great lesson of joy. Our family doesn't exactly follow the rules, and we don't use a point system; we play just to laugh. When each person gets their booklet back, we have a show-and-tell time and walk through all the drawings and guesses as they are revealed. The poor drawings and wild guesses results in some unexpected twists and turns—and some of the biggest laughs.

The reward from this game is the laughter we experience together. I have to confess that I have rarely laughed so much as when I have played this game.

In the Bible, we read of moments of joy and laughter. When Sarah and Abraham were told they would have a baby in their old age, Sarah laughed. At first she laughed in disbelief, but when her son was later born she laughed in joy and even named her child Isaac, which means "he laughs." Sarah said, *"God has brought me laughter, and everyone who hears about this will laugh with me"* (Genesis 21:6). She was able to look back and see great joy and hilarity in the situation when God had fulfilled His promise.

---

17 Tony Serebriany, *Telestrations* (Palmer Way, CA: USAopoly, 2009).

Sometimes we need a reminder that we just need to take the time to laugh and let go of the pressures of our projects, work, or life. We need to let go and see the humour in the situation.

Art Challenge

Create a series of drawings that you make in a limited amount of time. One to five minutes is more than enough time. Understand that the drawing will probably not be your best work, but let this time of creation alleviate any pressures or expectations you may have on yourself. Just draw and have fun. If you need ideas, here are a few you could draw: a person, an apple, a chair, a sunset, a pet, etc.

Order in Creation

READ ROMAN'S 1:19–20

> *For since the creation of the world God's invisible qualities—his eternal power and divine nature—have been clearly seen...*
>
> —Romans 1:20

I have always enjoyed the beauty of the world, particularly in nature. I grew up in the country and part of my upbringing included being able to walk through and explore the countryside. I've enjoyed photographing it, painting it, but also just breathing in the air and sweet scents and appreciating all that God has created for us in this world we live in.

Since I enjoy capturing this beauty in artwork, I was pleasantly surprised to learn about how we can see the hand of our God and Creator in the world. When paying close attention, a type of mathematical order seen in nature points to a creator. It's called the Fibonacci sequence and can be frequently be seen in the natural world.

The Fibonacci sequence is a series of numbers obtained from adding the two previous numbers to determine the next number in the series. The series 1, 1, 2, 3, 5, 8, 13... can be seen in the growth of a tree, the formation of pinecones, in shells, flowers, hurricanes, and waves. In many of these items, the sequence is seen in the formation of a spiral, called the Fibonacci spiral.[18]

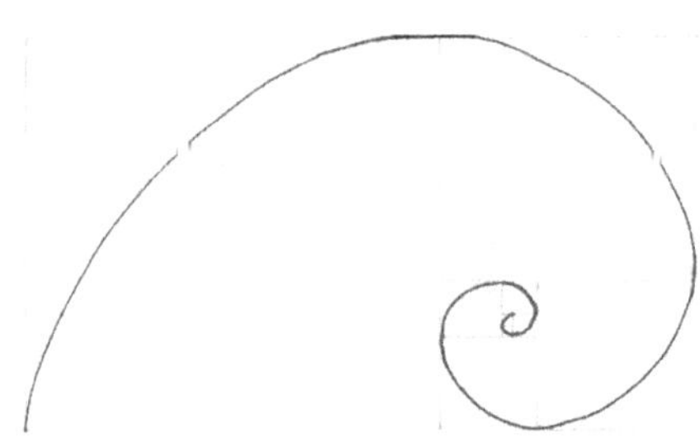

Squares drawn on a graph from a central point can help to draw the Fibonacci spiral.

The spiral is drawn by connecting squares in a spiral pattern, which is pictured here. The length of the sides of the squares follow the pattern of the sequence—1, 1, 2, 3, 5, 8, 13, 21, and 34. The spiral is then drawn by connecting the opposite corners of each square, beginning with the smallest square and moving outward with a curved line.

When this sequence was discovered and further explored, it was surprising to many to see the number of places where it appeared. However, knowing that our God is a God of order, it makes a great deal of sense. The Fibonacci sequence is just another imprint of God in the world He created.

---

18 "Fibonacci Number," *Wikipedia*. Date of access: December 27, 2019 (https://en.wikipedia.org/wiki/Fibonacci_number).

Art Challenge

Experiment with drawing the Fibonacci spiral in today's artwork. When you have the hang of it, try incorporating the spiral to create a wave or another item that uses this spiral shape. Surprisingly, if you have ever struggled with creating the perfect wave, this exercise could help you learn the skills you need to make it work.

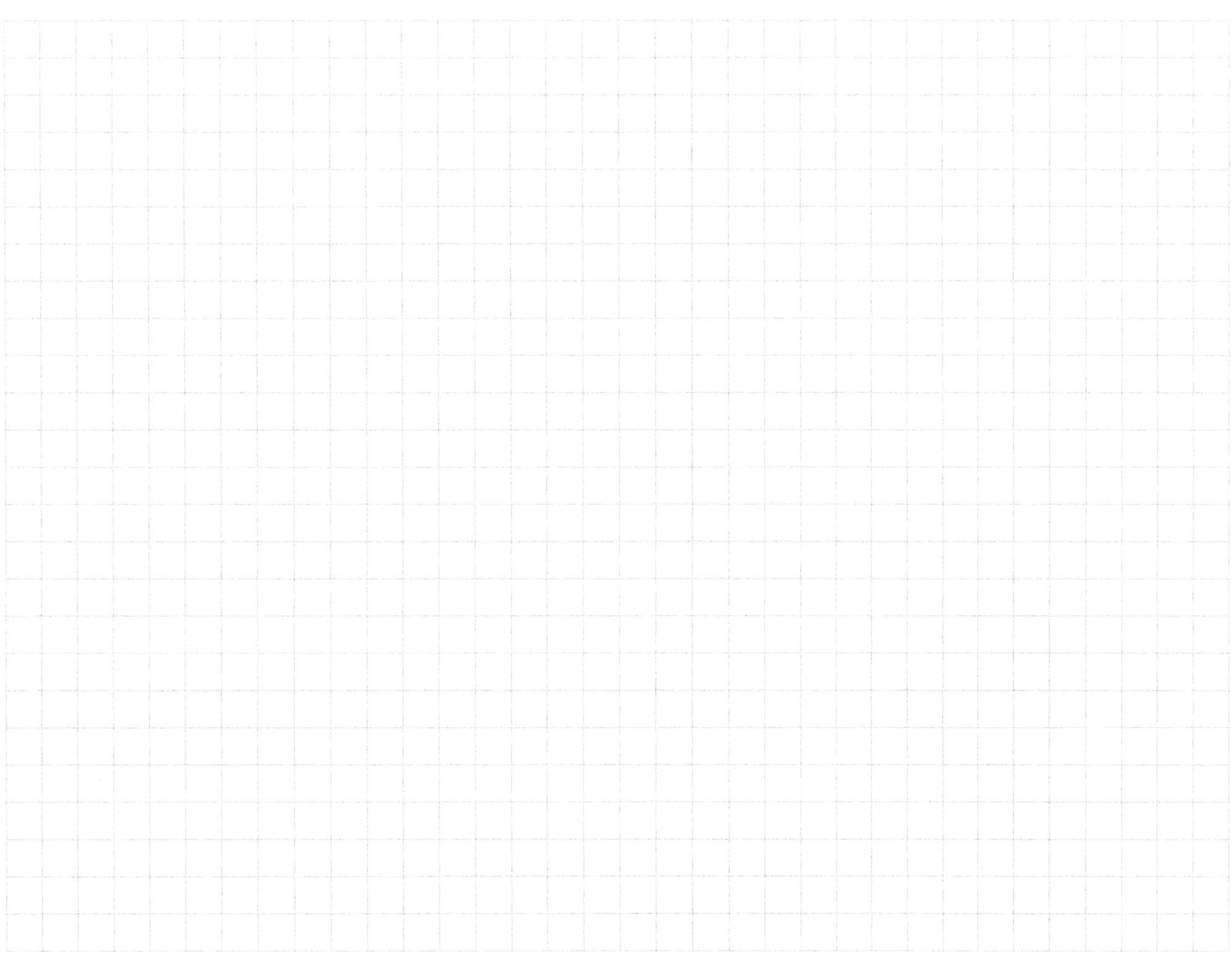

The Journey of the Midnight Flight

READ JOHN 21:15–19

Again Jesus said, "Simon son of John, do you love me?"

—John 21:16

I have been creating artwork since I was a child, but only recently have I started showing it. I've shown my artwork in shows where nobody bought anything. I've shown certain paintings several times but nobody seems to want them.

There is one painting, however, that has really made me appreciate the value of both patience and second chances. I created this painting ten or more years ago. I had the idea to paint a midnight sky, with the stars forming a subtle image of Jesus on the cross.

The painting didn't meet my expectations. I never showed it, and it sat there for many years.

About three years ago, I decided that I shouldn't waste the canvas, so I painted a big blue butterfly on it and left the midnight star background behind it. I showed it once, but nobody bought it. It seemed plain.

Then came my mixed media phase, where I decided to add black wire to highlight the veins in the wings and body, and I added some silver spirals and designs in the sky. I showed it twice and still got no interest. Or so I thought.

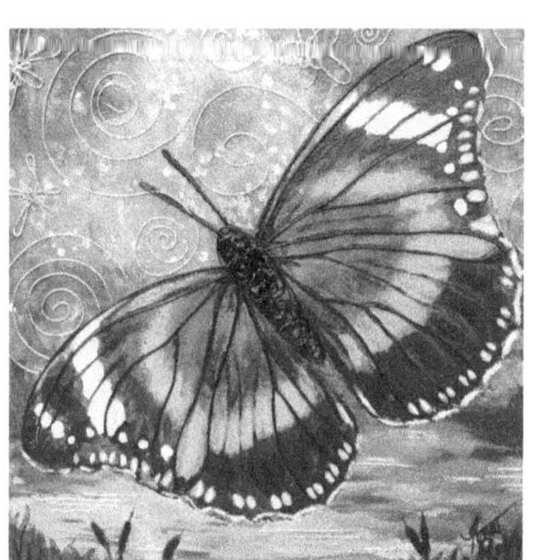

Midnight Flight
mixed media with acrylic and wire.

Six months later, I was contacted by a curator for an upcoming art show at our local university. She had seen the painting at a previous show and it had stood out to her enough that she asked for it by name among the thousands of pieces she had viewed across the city.

In preparation for the show, she wanted to do a write-up. We had the most amazing exchange. I learned that the school had been started by Ursuline Sisters, and that they still held very strong faith roots. The curator had chosen this painting because she had seen spiritual undertones in it. We were able to share with one another about our faith and the journey of the painting over the years.

The whole event was quite an experience, and at the end of the showing it ended up selling as well. If this painting had sold before, I never would have had the conversation with this curator. I never would have had this experience.

This painting had a second, third, and fourth chance in many ways, which made me think about how our God is a God of second chances. Peter is one of those we read about in the Bible who was given a second chance. After he denied Jesus three times, Jesus asked Peter if he loved him three times. Peter was forgiven for his faults and flaws and was reinstated by Jesus.

Remember that whatever your faults or flaws, you can be forgiven too. I am so glad that our God is a God of second chances.

Art Challenge

Is there a piece of artwork you've created that needs a second chance? Maybe you need to add something to it or start from scratch and try recreating a painting that didn't turn out before. An alternative idea would be to look at a previous devotion's drawing and give it a second attempt.

Detailed Art Challenge Activities

Approach passages as you did with "Scripture Meditation" devotional

Creative Reflection

But you are a chosen people, a royal priesthood, a holy nation, God's special possession, that you may declare the praises of him who called you out of darkness into his wonderful light.

—1 Peter 2:9

Supplies: For a simple design, use a fine tip marker and paper. To increase the creativity quotient, add a canvas and paint colours of your choice.

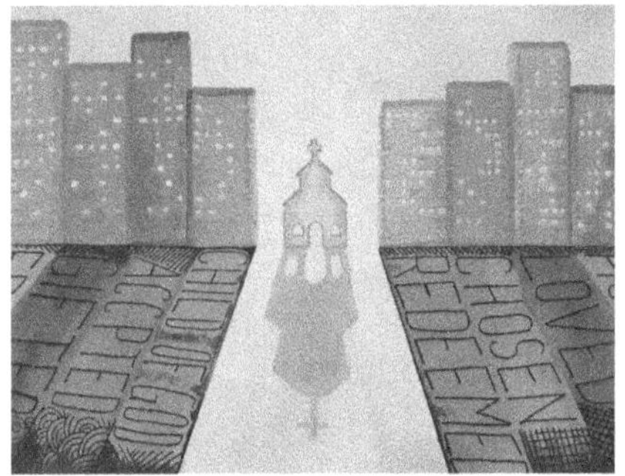

Sample of finished artwork

Begin by considering 1 Peter 2:9. What does it mean to you? You can artistically represent this verse in many ways. The artwork outlined here includes buildings to represent our nation, the church at the centre to represent us as His chosen people, and the shadows to show how we have been called out of the darkness and into the light.

Directions: Divide your canvas in half to create your buildings on the upper half and the shadows on the lower half. Begin by painting the background, making sure that the centre is the brightest, and slowly darken the background as you paint closer to the edges. When creating the buildings, use brighter colours. Use darker colours for the shadows but be careful not to make them too dark so that your marker will be visible when it is added later. Let your paint dry.

Choose a marker to outline your buildings and shadows. Make sure that your shadows angle outward to give a sense of light radiating from the centre of your artwork.

Inside the building shadows, add words that reflect how God sees you. They can be words you find in the Bible or they could be words that represent who God has called you to be.

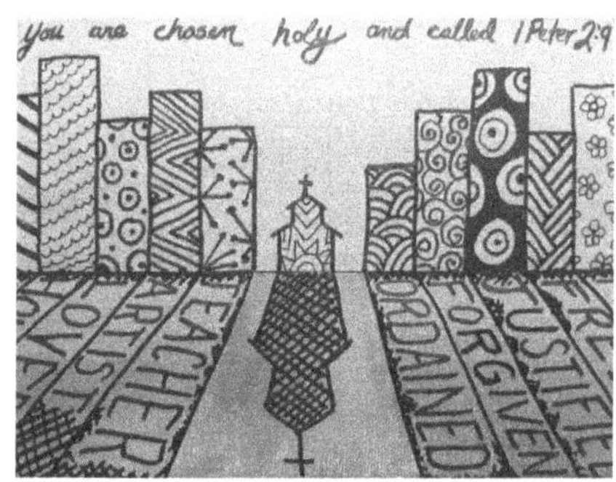

Alternate sample of finished artwork

Add details to the buildings. You can include windows, shading, or line patterns. Include the scripture in full or in part wherever you feel it suits your work best.[19]

19 Rev. Tina Rae, "CHOSEN | HOLY | CALLED; declaring the goodness of God," *live*, March/April 2019, 4.

Water-Themed Line Art

On the last and greatest day of the festival, Jesus stood and said in a loud voice, "Let anyone who is thirsty come to me and drink. Whoever believes in me, as Scripture has said, rivers of living water will flow from within them."

—John 7:37–38

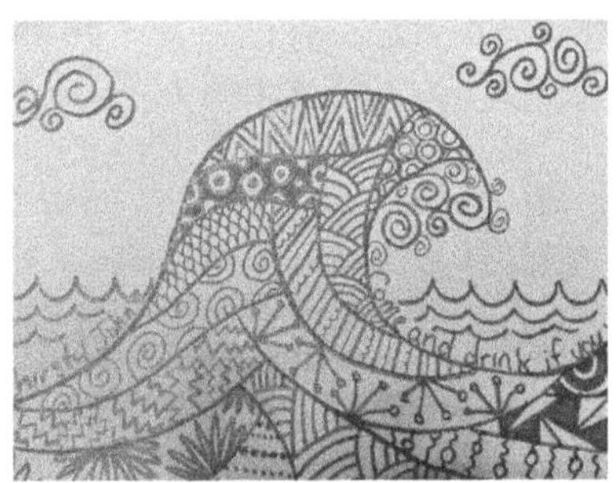

Completed art sample

Supplies: It can be as simple as a paper and a pen, or if you want more colour you can use a small painted canvas that has dried and add your design on top with a fine tip marker. Art can be an excellent way to express yourself and to meditate on God's Word.

I chose the above verses, paired with the theme of water, and reflected upon them to form this art project. As we proceed, you will create your artwork in a similar way.

Directions:

1. Choose a Bible verse to meditate on while working on your artwork. Later, you can incorporate this verse into your artwork. Choose one that is meaningful or speaks to you in a particular way. Feel free to use your favourite Bible translation too.
2. Verses that work well with a water theme are John 7:37–38, Genesis 1:2, Isaiah 12:3, Isaiah 43:2, 2 Samuel 22:17, Psalm 63:1, Revelation 22:17, and John 4:14.
3. Now that you've chosen your verse, let's get started on your artwork. To go with the theme of water, I've provided a barrel wave outline we will use as our starting shape. Draw your own or use the template that's included at the end of this devotion.

4. Divide up the space. There are many ways you can divide up the space within your wave. Here are two options to get you started.

   A braid pattern: start at the top and mark off a triangular tip. Each new curved line should start partway down on the last line and curve out toward the outer edge.

   A stripe pattern: start at the top and mark off a triangular tip. Continue making curved lines where the left edge is wider than the right edge.

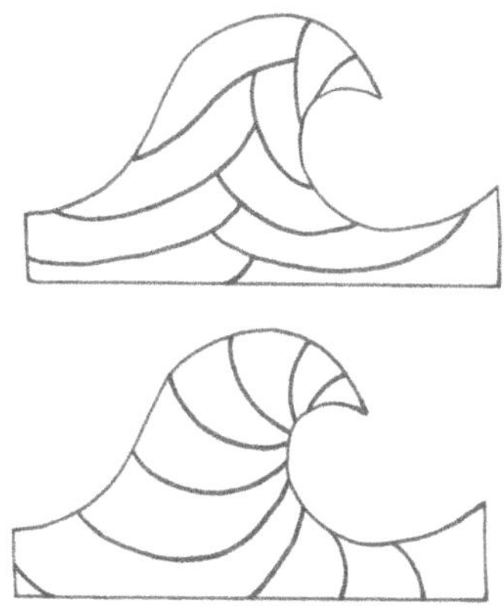

Completed art sample

5. Fill sections with patterns. Included are some examples of patterns.

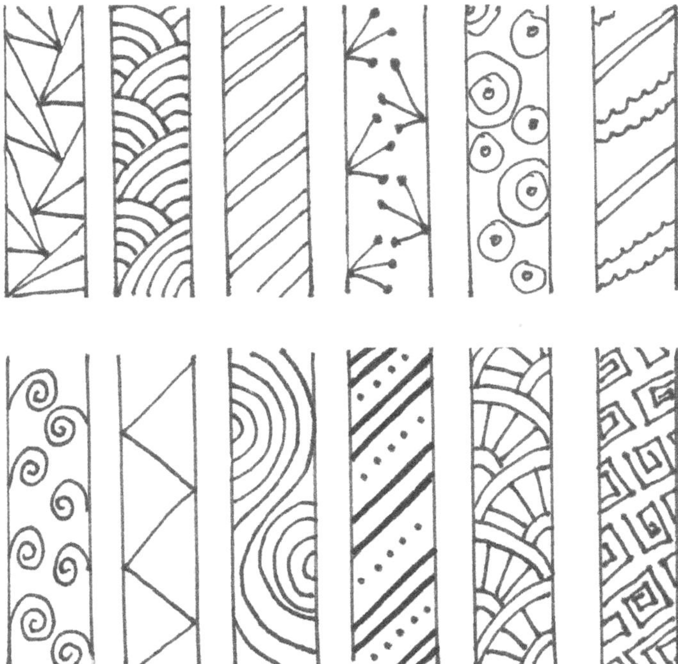

6. Add your scripture along the outside edge of your wave, inside one of your divided sections, or along the background waves.
7. Add your final details. Add background waves, with foam coming off your wave, some scripture, and draw some clouds.

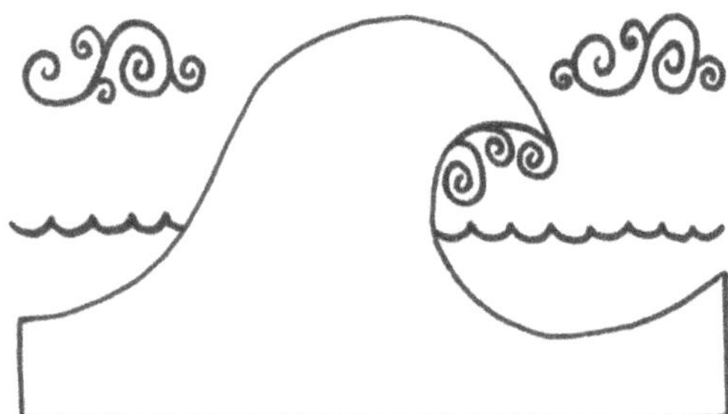

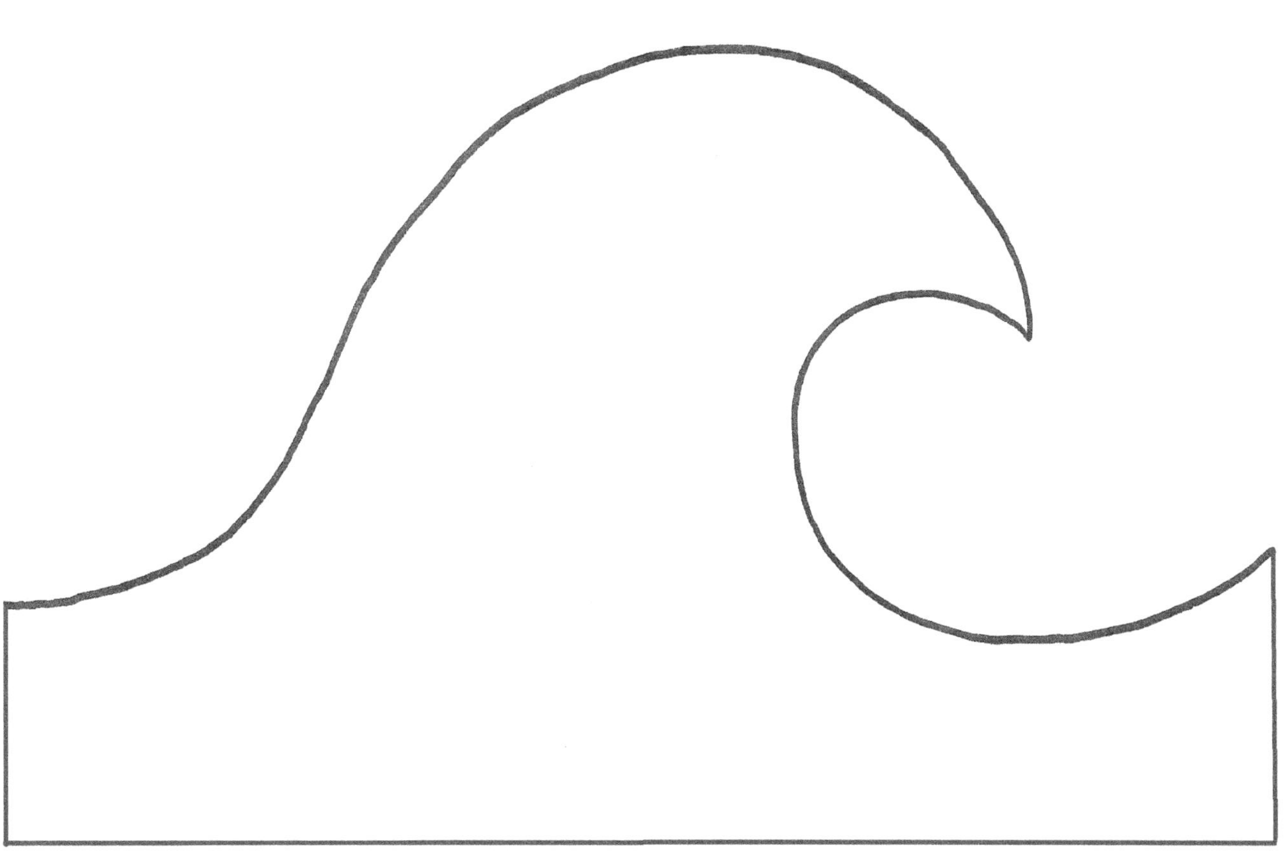

About the Author

Tina Rae is an ordained pastor with the Canadian Baptists of Ontario and Quebec and has been pastoring for fifteen years in Christian Education and Family Ministries. She is a wife and mother of two. As her kids have gotten older, she has loved getting deeper into painting and creating artwork.

Tina has shared her passion for faith and art within her church, with women's groups, and within her community. She is an executive member of the London Community Artists and has shown and sold her artwork in galleries and shows across Ontario.

www.ingramcontent.com/pod-product-compliance
Lightning Source LLC
LaVergne TN
LVHW061251100826
845148LV00008B/1100